New Business
in
INDIA
The 21st Century Opportunity

World Scientific Series on
21st Century Business : 1

New Business
in
INDIA

NEW BUSINESS
21st Century Opportunity

The 21st Century Opportunity

PAUL DAVIES
Onshore Offshore Ltd, UK

 World Scientific

NEW JERSEY · LONDON · SINGAPORE · BEIJING · SHANGHAI · HONG KONG · TAIPEI · CHENNAI

Published by

World Scientific Publishing Co. Pte. Ltd.

5 Toh Tuck Link, Singapore 596224

USA office: 27 Warren Street, Suite 401-402, Hackensack, NJ 07601

UK office: 57 Shelton Street, Covent Garden, London WC2H 9HE

Library of Congress Cataloging-in-Publication Data
Davies, Paul (Paul J.)
  New business in India : the 21st century opportunity / by Paul Davies.
    p. cm. -- (World Scientific series on 21st century business, ISSN 1793-5660 ; v. 1)
    Includes bibliographical references and index.
    ISBN-13: 978-981-279-042-2
    ISBN-10: 981-279-042-X
    ISBN-13: 978-981-279-044-6
    ISBN-10: 981-279-044-6
    1. India--Commerce--21st century. 2. India--Economic conditions.
  3. India--Social conditions. I. Title.
  HF3784.D38 2008
  658.1'10954--dc22

                                                    2008020250

British Library Cataloguing-in-Publication Data
A catalogue record for this book is available from the British Library.

Typeset by Stallion Press
Email: enquiries@stallionpress.com

Printed in Singapore.

For *Ruth, Phil, Alex and Phoebe*

ACKNOWLEDGEMENTS

I want to record my thanks to various people in India for their support and help and especially Selwyn Abraham and Suresh Chukkapalli. If ever I begin to think India and Indian business will defeat even me — they have unfailingly come to the rescue.

I also want to record my appreciation of Martin Palmer, the ace salesman, who over the years has taught me far more than I will ever be able to put into practice and who remains a constant inspiration.

CONTENTS

PREFACE

India — The 21st Century Opportunity and Why You Should be Part of It!

The world is witnessing something that has never happened before in so short a time. India, large in area and even more so in population, is developing so fast economically it is part of a transformation of the global economy. In a few short years, it has gone from middling failure to become a thrusting, dynamic business environment and is set to challenge the leaders in the world economy.

Inevitably there are questions about sustainability, about the social stresses and strains that massive economic growth can cause, and the impenetrability of what for so long was a virtually closed economy. My mission is to identify as many of the problems as I can and to show you how to overcome them, so you can gain the huge business benefits of being part of this exciting and once in a lifetime opportunity.

The vision behind this book is of an India integrated into the world economy, as both a supplier to and a customer of the rest of the world. It is already a major supplier of services and is becoming a major supplier of products, partly by buying major western companies. Achieving that vision will take determined efforts by western business — and that is what I want to encourage as the potential rewards represent the best opportunity for western business in the whole global economy.

India does still retain much of what westerners will regard as either its charm or its ability to frustrate. The use of English, for example, will bring a sparkle to your day — or leave you further in the dark. A billboard can announce in extraordinarily big type: *Sales 60% off — till all stocks last.* A traffic sign as you come out of Chennai airport would say something like the following in the West: *Slow — bridge works under progress.* In Chennai the actual sign says: *Slow bridge works under progress.* And when you point this out to an Indian, he or she will say that just shows how honest we are. As a collector and aficionado of these treasures of Hinglish – the combination of Hindi and English — my latest favourite is the admonition: *Accident Prone Area.* You know exactly what the author meant but it does convey the impression of a whole area collectively dropping tools on to its figurative feet and banging its putative finger nails instead of steel nails.

As for 'Avoid cellphone while driving' — I leave it to you but I just love the picture it creates in my mind.

I have covered a good deal of the quirks and treasures of Indian cultural life in my previous book, **What's this India business?**, which is focused on off-shoring and outsourcing to India. I cover most of the essentials of cross-cultural issues, including tipping, having a haircut and even an ayurvedic massage. Along with me you will still probably make the inevitable mistakes that trying to cross cultures entails, but I hope you can read and learn from the chapters in that book and be a little prepared for the shock that is India. I trust too that you will either come to love India, like I do, or at least see why I love it so much.

In the four years between these books not much has changed in the essential differences between western business cultures and India's quite unique business culture. The five-star hotels have gone from being a fabulous experience of customer service, and being expensive by any standards, to ruinously unaffordable. They are now filled with representatives of every western nation as opposed to the Brits and Americans and a sprinkling of Germans who were there when I wrote the previous book. There are, for example, even French nationals to be found, which is quite a turnaround in view of French attitudes to globalisation. There are also representatives of every one of what were the oriental tigers and the new entrants to the

European Union. In short India is the focus of an amazing amount of global business interest.

This is not just chance or a bubble of business interest, but a result of a fundamental shift in the global understanding of India and its burgeoning development into an economic force on the world stage.

From the West India is a very foreign country and yet most westerners will have a picture of what India is, gleaned from travel brochures, history lessons, geography studies, Bollywood movies, television documentaries and the Internet. It will be a confused picture because India is confused and confusing, with the modern, including a massively expanding economy, rubbing shoulders with an old India which is still very much alive in the villages.

Whatever you think about when India is mentioned, I want to introduce you to a new aspect of the country — its potential as a market for western goods and services and, indeed, for *your company's* goods and services.

I see India as the twenty-first century opportunity, which is a large claim, but I will show you why it is that tempting prize and how to be part of that opportunity.

India already has a high profile in business circles, for offshore call centres and IT development, for innovation, for its takeover of western companies, and its emergence as a world force in the global market. This book is part of the return compliment, recognising the huge potential of India as a market.

At the same time, for many people, India is hardly seen in those terms.

Our view of India is constrained by our various senses of geography, but as far as India is concerned, many of these perspectives are now history. It was once, three or four hundred years ago, a country of huge technological achievement, including the invention of zero. It is now fast becoming an economic powerhouse again. It was already a democracy at independence in 1947 but one that had the most rigid planning focused on self-sufficiency. It is still a democracy but one that is throwing off those shackles and is poised to achieve the greatest economic heights.

Geography is history in many senses. Where a country is determines a great deal of what happens in and to it. The successive invasions of India certainly determined a good deal of what the country was and is. The fact that the dominant language of business in India is English is but one example of that and the continuing legacy, good and bad, of the British Empire.

Yet in trying to understand how we think about India, its place in the world and how we should characterise its now apparently booming economy, we need to consider how geography is history in other ways.

In business terms, India's geographical location is not that important. It no longer really matters that India is some 5,000 kilometres from Europe or 7,000 miles from the US. If you can conduct a business process in the next office with the door closed, the advent of the Internet and high speed communications means that you can just as easily conduct that process anywhere in the world. If you also have a highly educated, relatively low paid work force, as India does, it makes good sense to put that process there. And as India is a democracy, has a rule of law, a free press and some 150 million people who speak, read and write the global language of business — English — it makes additional sense to put that process there.

Geography, finally, is history for India in a very disorienting way. (That word is particularly appropriate because *orient* is derived from the Latin word for the east — where the sun rose — and India is the East par excellence.) This view of geography is the most important for this book as so many of our attitudes have been determined by a rough and ready view of geography, particularly if you grew up like I did during the Cold War.

This understanding of geography focused on the main geographical axes: north and south, east and west.

For anyone over thirty, the east-west geographical opposition provided a range of certainties. The Cold War used this geographical concept to characterise the tension between Russia and the US and Europe. In this opposition, the East lost its sense of being exotic and mysterious and became threatening. In our binary political shorthand the West was *us* — democratic, innovative, dynamic, extrovert and market driven. The East was *them* — dictatorship, bureaucracy, introversion and a rigid planned economy.

India, despite being a democracy and in many ways having a western-oriented society, was often seen as part of that East. It looked to Moscow for arms, had a *licence raj* where business was hamstrung by restrictions of all sorts, and a highly protected economy.

After the Cold War, the East-West antagonism faded. India also nearly ran out of foreign reserves and in 1991 under the finance minister, Manmohan Singh, currently the Indian prime minister, India started to liberalise its economy. Tariffs were reduced, companies could be created relatively easily, the public sector was constrained and private enterprise encouraged. It was not quite as sudden a change as it might seem, as educational reforms had started in the early 1970s focusing on information technology, but by 1998, the West began to understand that India was becoming different. India was liberalised and the rigid stereotyping of East and West no longer really applied to India.

On the other hand, the stereotypes linger in people's consciousness far longer than the actual underlying facts and there is still political uneasiness in some areas about India. When you consider that Pakistan was our ally during the Cold War, and now has some very dubious connotations, you can see how the mind has to be flexible and accept new business realities.

The other axis, north and south, also provided certainties. Willy Brandt's commission in the 1970s characterised the world as north, rich, and south, poor. In that same binary political world north was *us* — rich — and south was *them* — poor. Africa and South America were essentially the south, but India was naturally easier to characterise with *them* despite being in the northern hemisphere. It had very low per capita income, suffered from declining world commodity and agricultural prices, and had a stagnant economy. It was, in what feels like an Orwellian phrase, a *developing country*, which essentially meant it was not developing at all and probably going backwards, at least relatively.

After achieving growth rates of between 6%–8% over the last five years, with some sectors of its economy, such as pharmaceuticals, information technology and business services achieving growth rates of between 20%–40%, India is breaking out of that geographical category of the south. While per capita income is still low, partly because of the sheer number of people — 1.1 billion — there is growing wealth in India that means that India is becoming a world economic force.

Once again, however, people's conceptions do not necessarily keep up with economic reality.

This creates an uneasy sense in Europe and the US so that we do not know whether India is north or south, part of *us* or part of *them* — whether India is a threat or an opportunity.

This book is designed to dispel that disorientation and to create what I see as the truer picture of India in business terms.

India has growing markets for goods and services and consumer goods, and few dominant suppliers in any of those markets.

On the other hand, India is a difficult market to enter. Corruption, bureaucracy, culture, customs, changing demographics, political unrest, and remnants of the *licence raj*, the system by which business was regulated out of existence, are just some of the reasons for this. There are specific business reasons too, for example, distribution of goods and understanding how to get through the regulatory traps are both challenging.

At the same time, India has one of the most customer-focused, reliable, efficient airlines in the world — Jet Airways, IT companies that inhabit modern marble palaces producing advanced solutions, and pharmaceutical companies developing cutting edge medicines.

Both these Indias exist side by side: the rich and the poor; the exotic and ancient and the technologically modern.

The booming, successful India where people still die because of drought. The India where female literacy can be below 40% in some states and yet in Kerala can be virtually 100%. The India where real estate prices can be some of the highest in the world, but when you land in the same Mumbai, the first sight is of the largest shanty town in Asia. The India where politicians rarely retire other than extraordinarily rich and people's needs are subordinated to personal gain, while imaginative and far-seeing legislation is put in place to preserve India's heritage. The India where *India Shining* was the election slogan of the most economically successful national government ever and yet the government was thrown out at the general election in 2004 because it was only true for a minority. The India that, over three centuries from 1500, produced with China half the world's wealth, but that in 1970 was barely able to feed itself.

The India that now delivers over 60% of the world's IT exports and, probably, over 70% of the world's business services exports, has the nuclear bomb, and some of the world's leading universities, yet has some 10% of its population in absolute poverty. The India of the *Kama Sutra* and world class medical research sitting on top of what may well be the largest, undiscovered HIV/AIDS pandemic and unable to confront the issue partly through prudery. The India which is welcomed into the global economy with relief and anticipation and the India which is seen as a major threat to the US and European economies.

It is no wonder that we find it extraordinarily difficult to characterise or even comprehend the booming Indian economy.

Despite the uneven distribution of the economic benefits, India is booming. There is, for example, a new, brand-conscious consumer market in India, driven by the export of jobs to India. The purchasing power of the upwardly mobile is growing daily. Even in real terms the wealth of this significant minority is worth knowing about. In 2008, there were more than one million people with annual incomes of over $300,000. This consumer market is a major development — and opportunity. Trickle down may not happen, but the economy is booming and some people are very rich there.

For me, welcoming India into the global economy, recognising the effects it will have on our economies and seeing the opportunities this new market will have for us, is most important — and we should characterise India as *us*, not *them*, and redraw the geographical concepts in our individual and collective minds.

For geography to become history properly, for India, and for Europe and the US, we have to characterise the new Indian economy in our minds and our business planning as a force for good and a major opportunity for the world — and especially the West.

And over the last two years more companies have been waking up to this opportunity and we have begun advising them how to enter the Indian market and be successful. Out of this day to day work, I have created this book. The most immediate opportunities are in the business to business sector, B2B, and this book is naturally focused more on this than the business to consumer, B2C, markets, but the opportunities in B2C are opening up extremely fast.

I hope this book reads like a conversation — inevitably one sided — but one where I detail the reasons why India is the twenty-first century opportunity for business. I will be explaining the difficulties and the issues and how to overcome them, or, more likely, short circuit them, and taking you through the thought stages you will have to confront if you want to establish your business in India. However much in love I am with India, I do understand the perils and the difficulties, and I hope that a clear eyed view of the whole opportunity is conveyed in this book.

I think most western companies of any size ought to make an informed decision about India as a market. You may well decide as a result of reading this book that the difficulties, the uncertainties and other reasons related to your own business mean that now is not the time for you to enter that market. That seems to me perfectly sensible as you have made it on the basis of the evidence.

On the other hand, I do also think that we need to grasp this amazing opportunity where we can.

Above all, I think that you should go to India to witness at first hand a dynamic business environment that is unparalleled. If you do that and you read this book and you still decide that now is not the time, I will naturally respect that decision — but a major part of me will be thinking that a great opportunity is being missed.

As you will see in these pages, I love India — and fell in love with the country and its business at first sight. The people are just amazing. I hope that I explain why — and that you find the book a challenge to any preconceptions you might have and a real spur to take up this opportunity.

And just when you begin to think that it is too daunting to get into India, keep in mind one rather comforting fact that I hope shines from this book. The barriers to entry into the Indian market are steep — and even steeper to those companies that come after you.

ONE

INDIA NOW

Whatever else you get from this book, by the end of it I hope you understand the excitement and the opportunity that India offers western business today. Of course India is a challenge and a thoroughly strange and exotic environment and you should just go there and see at firsthand what a dynamic business culture it has. Now is exactly the right moment to go there and make a reasoned decision whether you are going to enter that market and exploit the opportunity it presents or to stay your hand for the moment. The second message from this book is that now may not be the right time for your company to enter that market but there is a real imperative for you to make a soundly based decision and not let the opportunity slip through your fingers. The market is growing so fast, it just should not be ignored.

We are witnessing in India one of the fastest and most complete transformations of an economy that the world has ever seen. What took something like forty or fifty years in the West, is going to happen in not much more than a few months in India or it will at least seem like that.

There are losers in this process, within the Indian economy and within the world economy. In five years the retail shopping environment is going to be transformed, as multinational companies and larger and larger Indian retailers effectively destroy the living of a vast number of small retailers.

1

More and more semi-skilled and highly skilled workers in the West are being marginalised by competition from India. (The really unskilled are not so badly affected as they generally do the jobs like fruit picking that cannot — at least yet — be done three or six thousand miles away.)

In that same revolution, however, there are going to be winners and this book is focused on how to be part of that winning environment.

To take a prosaic example and one that gives a real insight into what is happening in India at a more profound level, look at the rise of road transport. Of course India's roads have been full for years. The spectacularly dilapidated, colourful and grindingly slow trucks that have trundled across India, overloaded, hand painted, home to the driver, and competing for every inch of road space with cockroaches — the three wheeler motorised rickshaws — bicycles, cars, bullock wagons and cows, have been a picturesque and precise image of the infrastructure problems in India. At least 50% of their time is seemed to be spent waiting. Waiting for traffic to clear, waiting for controls to be cleared, waiting to pay *octroi*, the tax on goods passing between states, waiting for something to happen.

Like the electricity supply in India, trucking certainly existed, more or less as an afterthought. Like the postal service, the truck would get there eventually, and as long as time was not of the essence, it was quite reliable. But it did take an age in doing so.

So the change to road transport in this current decade in India is breathtaking and a symbol of the energy, investment, focus, and the ability to create and then transform a muddle that is India. The Golden Quadrilateral is one of the biggest indicators of change in India. Nearly 6,000 kilometres of dual carriageway, or interstates, linking Delhi, Mumbai, Kolkata — previously known as Calcutta, and Chennai — previously known as Madras, have almost all been built and will form a sort of quadrilateral and change the face of India. Already being widened from four to six lanes, both to meet and to stimulate demand, the project was worth over $12 billion when first conceived in the late 1990s.

What it will actually cost is quite amazing in a country that many people in the West regard as just an emerging economy. The development of something approaching modern road transport is happening in India before our eyes.

2

Most importantly, a process of developing modern, high speed roads that started in Europe and the US in the 1930s and was only brought to anything like a finished state in the 1980s some fifty years later, is going to be accomplished in less than 10 years.

Being able to drive between the metros — or largest cities — in India is almost mind boggling. In fact it is almost as mind boggling as the idea of venturing today on to Indian roads, no matter how modern, for any westerner.

For those of us who have watched India over the last decade, understanding the scale of investment, not just of money but of political and economic will, is what gives the biggest indicator of the new India and the new business in India. You will often hear people suggest that because India is a democracy and there are so many competing interests, nothing much can be accomplished in India. If you understand that sentiment and are used to the usual Indian approach of making do, waiting, shrugging, and generally concluding, after a considerable gap, that will do for now, the physical advent of the Golden Quadrilateral is what is most staggering. It is little short of a cataclysmic change in approach, understanding and capability.

Of course there are worries about corruption in awarding the contracts. Of course there were delays as the states decided whether or not to work with the Union government. Of course the whole thing looked like a shambles even beyond the point that the roads themselves were pressed into use. And yet the roads are being used.

This development of the Golden Quadrilateral has another message. It was the opportunity to be a supplier to such a gargantuan project that changed a significant number of business attitudes in the developed world and made the question of whether to enter the Indian market very much more pressing and significant.

More important than any of this however is how indicative of the new India this is — and how indicative of the wholesale changes that are going on in the sub continent. Taken on its own the Golden Quadrilateral is symptomatic. Taken as part of a more holistic view it is astonishing.

Twenty years ago there would have been almost no understanding in India of the use that such a road infrastructure might have, let alone any concept of building it. Now it is an essential element in the development of India that will create, support, stimulate, develop and reinforce a completely new consumer and business market in the world. Alongside it is the development of an amazing air passenger industry.

Jet Airways broke the mould in India, providing exceptional customer service and, even more alarming to those of us used to travelling in India on Indian Airlines, punctuality. Now Jet is fighting for every seat against a host of new competitors, including Kingfisher which is providing a most effective competitive threat. We are also seeing the advent of the low cost airlines, picking up the model of South West Air, EasyJet and Ryan Air. In a few years, from a rather comfortable — from the airline's point of view — position of arriving whenever it suited the airline, cancelling flights on what looked like the merest whim, serving the oddest combinations of food, and treating passengers as being privileged enough just to be flying at all, the market has been transformed.

Now that the private Indian airlines have started to go international, the world of Indian aviation has been doubly transformed. At the launch of Jet's new international first class, with its separate cubicle for each passenger and, of course, a proper flat bed, the sight of two Bollywood stars disappearing through the cubicle door together and then closing it behind them caused quite a few ripples, mainly of disapproval. Whatever that might have portended, there is no doubt that Indian travel and transport is changing rapidly, in quality, opportunity and in breadth.

If we stick with road traffic in India for a moment, it is as well to see the roads as very much a metaphor for Indian business and how it operates in the domestic market. It can be both fast and furious and deadly and slow. On the one hand there is the exhilarating speed of Delhi. Like a great deal of Indian domestic business, it rushes at breakneck speed, and is as entrepreneurial as each person grabs a new part of the road space and makes it his or her own. Then there is the gridlock of Mumbai, where competing interests and a lack of incentive to give up an inch of space ensure that traffic moves hardly at all and it is difficult to imagine getting anywhere. If you can keep those two contrary pictures in your head at the same time, you can probably make sense of what it is to do business in India — the good and the bad.

4

Just when you thought the open road lies ahead, some restriction will be placed in your way. In my own case opening my own company in Chennai was blissfully straightforward. Not one of my professional advisers could think of any issues that might arise. Then I ran into the full spectrum of constraints. I could not have the name I wanted because anything that dealt with onshore and offshore was obviously to do with the oil industry and therefore I had to put up working capital of outrageous sums. From this rather strategic objection, I hit problem after problem, even down to the place where the UK notary public put his seal on my documents. His seal and signature were unexpectedly, apparently, at the bottom of the page. This rendered all the documents null and void. It was not the cost — though that was substantial — but the time and effort that had been expended getting the documents together at all that really rankled.

In short, never relax in Indian traffic or in Indian business, never take your eye off the slightest detail — because something will be lurking to grab you and change all your time scales.

More than being symbolic, the massive developments in infrastructure in India are part of the transformation of a significant number of Indian lives. Adding another 250 million consumers to the world economy is impressive enough to grab attention and that is about the number out of the 1.1 billion Indians that already have some access to the world economy. When that 250 million are predominantly under 30, with large, and growing, disposable incomes, a world view formed by television and, more significantly, the Internet, well able to use English, the language of international business, accustomed to free speech, the rule of law, and learning to enjoy freedom from bureaucratic control — the result is going to be amazing.

The markets that I am most comfortable with in India are predominantly business to business, or B2B, rather than the business to consumer, B2C, markets. If I take one small example that is dealt with in more detail later, you will see why this is the first growth area. Car production is increasing very fast in India, but a large proportion of the new cars being produced is exported. Providing car components to the factories producing the cars is clearly an interesting market, as is providing the elements necessary for the production of car components. There are growing B2C markets, but first look at the B2B opportunities.

Nevertheless, the money that these new members of the global consumer society have is the key to the future of the domestic market in India. When I was managing director in India there were suggestions about the difference in salary between me and my Indian staff. The discussion centered on the amount of money going in the two different directions. My six figure salary in pounds sterling was often a matter of wild speculation — and I wish I had earned the amounts that were being suggested — but even unquantified it was thought of as riches beyond the thoughts of avarice. Against that my managers compared their own four and very low five figure salaries.

My approach to dealing with the issue was to talk about purchasing power and standard of living.

It was agreed, of course, that they each had a driver paid for out of their miserably low salaries. They each had at least one maid. (There was usually at this point some shuffling and embarrassment because I did not realise that it was at least two maids. It was, of course, further evidence that I did not understand.) They did have a gardener — well, only if they had a garden, it was pointed out.

I revealed in return that not only did I not have a driver in the UK, but that, despite possessing a garden, I had no gardener. This was frankly a bit far fetched of course. The fact that we did not have even one maid was however so astonishing that it tested their belief in my truthfulness. As this conversation did not just happen once but on reasonably frequent occasions, it was obviously deeply shocking and unbelievable.

My veracity was tested by asking whether I had children? Many. *And you didn't have a maid?* No. *Who changed the diapers or nappies?* When I said me, it was like watching the heroine of a Jane Austen novel who, through too much exposure to peasant life, had to lie down all afternoon with the vapours, as they struggled to deal with this impossible fact.

I had to modify my answer by saying that it was my wife if I was not in the house, but this caused almost as much disbelief.

The discussion always progressed to the real point, which was the difference in purchasing power. Out of my salary, in an average year, there was

6

nothing left over after, admittedly, a reasonable standard of living. My senior managers, by contrast, all married with families and the usual household and educational bills, had money left over to spend on non essentials, and that was after paying for all their family retainers.

A few years on, with salary inflation having been quite extreme in parts of Indian business, and looking at a cross section of employees in the off-shoring world and even within parts of the domestic Indian economy, it is possible to see that India's domestic market is becoming very attractive to western business. Where else in the world will you find such a growing cohort of globally aware consumers with money to spend?

Purchasing power in India makes it the fourth largest economy. They might still be hyper-sensitive about price — and they are — but they have disposable cash. They also have demands, and their exposure to western goods, whether in books, magazines, television or primarily from the Internet, is more than sufficient to begin to overwhelm domestic supply. They are real, first generation consumers of electronics, entertainment, experience and pleasure.

The contrast with China, for example, is stark because the single child policy has really limited the number of people of working age and the age profile of the population is very different from India. The number of dependents that each wage earner has to support is growing fast in China, but in India it is still shrinking.

The sheer quantity of people in India who have money to spend has grown, their awareness of global brands is increasing daily, and the demand for consumer goods has grown immensely. It is still very difficult to address the end consumer in India but the opportunities for selling into the businesses that supply those consumers become more and more attractive.

In addition there is another fact of Indian life that is going to speed up the transformation that I have been outlining so far.

If you consider the amount of energy that Indian business people have devoted to working their way round, through, under and across a stifling bureaucracy, you will begin to understand how much of an impact Indian business people will have on the world as the controls are loosened. That statement is made in the full knowledge of how successful they have been on a world business stage already. The percentage of the world steel production that is owned by Indians is already significant. The dominance of the world information technology development budget is well known. But we have not really seen the power of India and Indian business.

When the restrictions in the internal market are removed — gradually and painfully slowly at times — the energy Indian businesses will unleash on the world will be astonishing. As one small example, take the telecoms industry. It was one of the first business areas to be liberalised. Now every month some five million extra mobile phones are added to the consumer base in India. That is staggering number even when you say it quickly.

This development helped convince me that once India starts to move in business and throws off bureaucratic constraints, it becomes unstoppable.

The opportunity of selling into such a new, vast market is very difficult to grasp. The inevitable downside is that each unit will be sold for a very low value in the foreseeable future. Yet the upside remains that the volumes that are possible are immense. The important additional factor is that creating a market presence is relatively inexpensive compared with any western market and the very real risks are relatively easy to understand and deal with as they are nearly all within the Indian domestic market itself.

This means that while growth in India will be fuelled by the global economy, its huge domestic economy will provide enough insulation to carry on even if the world economy falters.

If there is no other message from this book, then bear this one point in mind. Many people think that current economic development in China is underpinned by state-directed, inefficient loans producing an unbalanced and bubble-like economy. If this bubble bursts and leads to, if not a collapse, a recession and the re-establishment of the Chinese economy on sounder lines, India may well be affected along with the rest of the world. The difference is that it will not remove the fundamental strengths of the Indian economy, especially as energy sources, whether pipelines from Russia or domestic discoveries of oil and gas, are made more secure. The momentum in the Indian market is not entirely self-sustaining and completely safe from down turns in the global economy, but it is remarkably strongly based and has a banking infrastructure largely determined by market forces.

On the other hand, I do not want to disguise the fact that there are, nevertheless, all sorts of problems in dealing with India. There are extremes of uneven development, an economy with enough imbalances to cause social unrest, and massive variations across the country which is, after all, a sub-continent if not *the* sub-continent. Even if the fundamentals are simply astonishing, and the opportunity vast, there are many traps for the unwary. As this book develops you will see more of them, but let me bring one or two into focus here to counterpoint the idea that India is in any sense a monolith. I recognise the real differences across the country and the fact that while the opportunities are great viewed across the sub-continent as a whole, in different areas and different parts of the economy there may well be no real opportunities for western companies.

The individual states in India, most of them bigger than the average European Union country, have jealously guarded their freedom and independence. It is true that sales tax at different rates is at last being replaced by VAT imposing some uniformity. Border customs posts between states are becoming far less important but there are still hold ups at the crossing points. Television, another industry being liberalised, is cross border. The Internet is cross border. Businesses are located across the country, but you will still become aware of the roots of each business and understand that a Maharashtran company — typically from Mumbai — will have a different approach from one that originated in Tamil Nadhu.

If I take one key issue, you will see the impact that the regional and state differences have and how, while it is possible to see India as a unified state, at a business level, it is best to be aware of local differences. Female literacy, the silver bullet in social, political and economic development, is probably very close to 100% in Kerala, a state in the south. If the mother is literate, there is a good chance that the children will be — and the focus of the family will be towards education and development. In Bihar, a poor northern state, female literacy is said to be about 40%, and as you cannot trust the statistics compiled by state officials who are subject to real political pressure, even 40% is likely to be an exaggeration.

This gender difference in literacy has a profound impact on the potential of each state, and should be assessed carefully. It probably matters more than any other indicator for assessing the long term opportunities in any particular state, and yet it is not one of the key indicators in most business assessments.

For me this leads into an understanding of attitudes in India. As with all places, attitudes in India, even within the most progressive parts of the business world, do not keep pace with structural and business changes. Attitudes are being transformed but working in the Indian market is like living in a geological map with different layers of consciousness.

At the highest level you will deal with people with the greatest confidence, aware of their world class skills and comfortable with them. You might be in India, you might be in Dallas — it would not matter. At a different level, even with the educated people you will be dealing with directly when setting up in India, you will find extremes of naivety and roguery, inferiority complexes, arrogance, and total insecurity.

In many ways this is not that much different from any other business culture. In India, however, this will be coupled with one of the biggest cross cultural divides for westerners, which is very difficult to understand let alone deal with until you are acclimatised to it. There is an apparent gentleness and lack of aggression in Indian business life. It is more apparent than real, but it can lull even the most astute western business person into a false sense of security. As with all cultural issues, the only safeguard is not to trust your instincts.

Placing the people you are dealing with within this geological social structure is as difficult as reading body language and subtleties across cultures. The danger is more extreme, however, than that. You just have to remember that Indian business people will be far more used to western culture through television and other media than you will be to understanding Indian business culture. The opportunities for disaster are great. If you start to feel comfortable with someone in India in a relatively short period of time and you have only a limited amount of experience of India, warn yourself to be on your guard. It is entirely possible that the person you are dealing with is adopting western approaches and words. This may be entirely helpful and genuinely based on a desire to make you feel at home, but my rule is that the more comfortable you feel, the more wary you should be.

10

In a sense this is just general advice for anyone going from one business culture to another, but it is more than that as India is such a patchwork of attitudes, different perspectives and regional variations. It is doubly tempting to see India as a monolith and comprehensible as it is almost too difficult to deal with otherwise. Watch yourself carefully.

Hidden Benefits and Hidden Costs

Overview

It is relatively easy to stumble badly when working with India and not only because of the cultural differences and the different approach to business. In addition to those very real twin perils, you will find that there are any number of hidden costs and business issues that will hit you unexpectedly. If you are not prepared properly and the hidden costs do strike home, then the undoubted hidden benefits of working with India will pale into insignificance.

You may be partly prepared for the existence of hidden costs by the various stories about working offshore which are becoming urban myths. While you are getting to understand the offshore world, you will probably often hear that many of the business processes that went overseas are coming back to the West. The unstated presumption will be that this is happening because the promised benefits did not materialise and the hidden costs defeated everything people tried to do. You may even find people who will quite authoritatively state that data protection is such a huge and undefined problem that no one can actually deal with it effectively in India. If that does not scare everyone, from the opposite end of the spectrum, there are people who will proclaim that your country's domestic employment legislation will follow you to the ends of the earth with disastrous results. You may even hear horror stories of people getting the service they specified but with calamitous results as their specification was so full of holes.

As with all urban myths there is probably a grain of truth behind every story, especially the latter, in just the same way that inevitably some Indian call centre workers must watch the odd western soap so they can chat author-itatively to western clients. Yet these examples of the generation of fear, uncertainty and doubt, the well-known *FUD* factors, are not what should be in the forefront of your mind when contemplating going offshore to India. The real hidden costs are worth examining in detail as a preparation to realising the equally real hidden benefits of going offshore.

Some of these hidden costs will seem obvious once they have been intro-duced, but it is worth saying that many companies have gone offshore with-out the first thought about them. If you remember that ordinary, domestic outsourcing projects often fail, up to 50% according to Gartner, the industry analysts, and that there are a good deal more variables going offshore, it would not be surprising that the failure rate can be even higher going to India.

Hidden Costs

In any offshore exercise for a company of any size whatsoever, whether out-sourcing or entering the Indian market, you will quite properly find your pro-curement department involved. It may be that you will be selecting suppliers of local goods or professional firms to provide you with legal or accounting services. There are two issues leading to hidden costs here, and although they sound contradictory at first, they are, in fact, complementary.

The first is that your procurement department will not initially know much about going offshore or specific country issues. The second is that many if not all of your potential Indian suppliers will know a great deal about western procurement practices. The result is that your procurement depart-ment will be faced with a difficult task that will appear in practice to be quite straightforward with an obvious answer. The corollary is that they will find it extraordinarily difficult to differentiate between or appreciate those Indian companies that are not as geared up to meet western procurement expecta-tions and which will therefore seem quite alien. Thus when they are pre-sented with a company that seems to be very normal and comfortable and just what your procurement department is used to, the result is usually predictable and, equally usually, unsatisfactory.

12

The first important hidden cost in any offshore procurement is therefore either training members of your procurement department in how to deal with what is an alien business culture or employing a consultancy which is experienced in dealing with these issues. Cynics will, probably rightly, explain that selecting just the right consultancy for your business is an additional cost. If the cost is not apparent in money terms, it will be in time and that is often just as important.

And if you involve your procurement department in the process for selecting the consultancy, you still might be in a muddle. You can see from this how the hidden costs can mount up.

If you do not train your procurement staff in how to address the differences when dealing with offshore suppliers; or use bought in expertise, you will find that your supplier selection process, no matter how apparently objective and strategic and inexorable, will not give you the results you need. It will, however, give your potential Indian suppliers, who are aware of how procurement works in the West, what they want.

This example illustrates a real truth about many of the hidden costs and issues in going offshore. If you always keep in the back of your mind that offshore companies probably understand you better than you understand them, you will have a much better perspective and approach. To summarise this, you need to be able to see the difference between a company that has worked hard to understand you in order to provide you with just the right solution for your needs, and a company that will tell you what it knows you will find easy to hear and appreciate. This might seem no different from your experience with potential suppliers in your domestic market. It is quite different, however, once you see how attractive and compelling the latter proposition will seem when every other supplier appears so alien.

On any number of occasions I believe that we have more than earned our consultancy fees just by being able to demonstrate to my western clients what is actually happening in front of their eyes and ears, as opposed to what they are perceiving.

The second hidden cost in this area — often hidden because it does not figure in any budget as it occurs too early in the process — also relates to this selection of an Indian supplier or partner. For many years I have focused on the criteria for selecting a supplier whether in one's home market or abroad, and selecting one across cultures is especially fraught. Do not be tempted, however, to cast your net wider and wider when faced with the difficulty of choosing a supplier or partner in the belief that by doing so you will reduce risk or that you will get a better understanding of the criteria you must use.

You will only pile cost on cost.

There is a real example of an insurance company that started by seriously considering over 200 suppliers, and that was only after desk work had reduced the initial list to that number. This is obviously absurd and was actually worse than it looks, because this in-country exercise only kicked in after an exhaustive process of identifying India as the right country.

Any number of major western companies have abandoned their normal approach and created short lists of 20 because they do not have the tools to differentiate effectively between companies. I have come to the conclusion that this means two things: that the western company does not trust Indian companies and also does not trust its ability to select.

There are simpler and much more cost-effective ways of going through this process and if you do not trust Indian companies or your own company to get the right answer, then it is probably better to abandon the process before you start.

A large cost in entering an offshore market, and one that will not immediately appear to be hidden, is travel to your chosen country. The reason why it becomes a hidden cost is that it is so often under-estimated. Western business people's travel and subsistence costs in even, say, India, are such that it does not take much extra travel for your original budget to look decidedly optimistic. This is, of course, without considering opportunity costs associated with senior managers being out of the office.

Rather than detail the way that extra travel usually builds up, which is fairly obvious, let me look at ways of mitigating those extra costs. There are some straightforward and legitimate approaches that will immediately save you money, such as, for example, buying air fares in India. The cost differential is surprisingly large. If, for example, you have two return journeys to make in a limited time, buy the middle trip, from and to India, in India.

Try above all to avoid ad hoc trips. This is quite normal advice, but somehow India traps even the wary into making more and more unplanned trips. It is partly to do with the way that meetings are generated and held at short notice in India. Inevitably, too, during a project ad hoc trips will become what the project team calls essential. Such trips are usually very expensive, not only because you have to buy the tickets at short notice, but because they are incredibly disruptive. You will find that while someone is offshore putting out some forest fire other problems will build up at home. You will lose time and you will lose momentum. Going into India often multiplies the number of ad hoc trips and increases the costs dramatically.

It is best to take a more strategic approach to reducing travel costs and budget for them properly in the first place. If that sounds counter-intuitive, it is — but it also reflects a great deal of experience of dealing with India.

In your planning phase make some allowance for these trips in your budget, but much more importantly work out a plan to reduce them to the minimum. You may find that once your in-house project team has worked out what it is doing and how it will do it, that is a good time to make a team trip. It may not be appropriate for your circumstances, but I have seen an apparently huge up-front cost for a team visit pay dividends. These benefits come largely from the shared understanding that is usually created not only within the team but also with third parties.

We all know, for example, that a phone call to a person that you have met face to face is incredibly more productive. That does not change across cultures and, in fact, it becomes even more important.

I made the point about budgeting properly for this cost line. Whatever you do, do not turn an expected and important, overt cost into a hidden one by underestimating how much travel will inevitably cost. You should allow something over $7,000 per week, including business class air fares and subsistence, for a trip.

I am by nature a pessimistic business planner and always try to allow for more travel than seems reasonable. If you take a more optimistic view of travel requirements, you would not need many surprise trips to ruin your budget, and those surprises always happen.

Having expatriates in-country is often rightly seen as an essential way to establish your company offshore and it will not initially look like a hidden cost as it will appear quite properly in your projected budget. It will often become a hidden cost, as it will usually be more expensive than it looks. This is not just because, for example, real estate rents are very high in the metros because this can be allowed for. The hidden costs are actually subsidiary to that and insidious in my experience.

Let me give one real example. Having that expatriate, even if absolutely essential, will provide a magnet with inevitable results. He or she will have to be reviewed. He or she will need back up. There will be any number of reasons why a trip is necessary and some of these will be genuine and valid. If you eliminate such subsidiary trips, you will probably suffer in business terms. The answer is not to underestimate the extra travel that will be generated by having your own person on-site.

There are other costs that also become hidden costs if they are not properly appreciated. You will readily understand them and you can probably anticipate them but you first have to be aware of the possibility. Even so, these can easily move from open costs to hidden costs. Training, for example, will obviously be important, and you will probably very happily concentrate on training people in your processes and procedures and, to some extent, appreciate that you have to train people to understand your domain issues. Translating that training into productive work will broadly take the same amount of time as in your home country. As you will probably be employing very intelligent and more highly qualified staff than at home, you will find that they will make astonishing initial progress, but you will find that the moment when real understanding is achieved and the time when hidden benefits start to accrue takes longer than onshore. It will not just be your processes and procedures that are new to your Indian staff, but the whole environment and your business culture.

Look carefully at recruitment costs, too, especially as these may impact your costs in an unexpected way. Recruitment in the Indian information technology world, and now in the business process outsourcing world, is slick and brilliant, relying on networks of people who can find the right skills quickly. It works astonishingly well. This will lead any Indians that you involve in the early stages of your business development in India to underestimate the amount of time and effort that will be required for effective recruitment. We have recruited for a range of clients in India and it can be a long and protracted process, not least because you will not be well placed to assess the capabilities of the Indians presented to you.

My advice is always be wary about projected recruitment costs for any business that you will establish in India.

My last hidden cost here is focused on scale. If you are entering the Indian market, you will know that you cannot in all likelihood take on the whole of India in one go. You will need to focus on one metro or state at first. The hidden cost arises when you do not enter the market properly. There is a tendency to take a small step and imagine that you can then learn from that and take bigger and bigger steps. My experience is that this does not work and causes no end of extra costs that cannot be allowed for in such planning. There is no substitute for entering the Indian market at what you believe is a self-sustaining level. You have to be big enough to make an impact and you have to be big enough from the outset to have a fully functioning operation. If this sounds self-evident, there are any number of companies that have dipped what they call their toes in the water and then more or less floundered before pouring in extra resources in an unplanned and haphazard way.

The paradox for me is that the actual costs of entering the market in sufficient size are not that much greater than entering the market piecemeal or tentatively. Then over time, the costs of getting the organisation up to a sensible, sustainable size overwhelm the initial budget and this hidden cost will threaten the very success of the endeavour. As you will see in this book, the financial costs of entering the Indian market are not the real barrier to entry, so if you are going to be part of the Indian market, remember that size really does matter and ensure that getting to the right size does not involve major hidden costs.

A good measure is to understand what the costs will be of entering the market in what you know is sufficient scale. If those costs seem excessive compared to your understanding of the rewards, you will know that you should qualify out. It is without doubt entirely wrong to enter the Indian market below the scale that you know has to be present for you to succeed, and that includes all the costs of after sales service, training, and getting through a bureaucracy that will at first seem impenetrable.

Other hidden costs will not be that different from those of any project. There may be cost over runs on individual items. There may well be — almost certainly will be — the usual costs from delays and unexpected hitches. These may be more significant because it is in India, but they would not be any different in type.

In this light, as an introduction to hidden benefits, let me introduce the hidden costs involved in understanding your own processes. In the absence of a good reason to believe otherwise, I have always found that it is sound business practice when establishing your company in India to impose your standards, processes and procedures on your Indian subsidiary. There will be localisation and some degree of flexibility, but one of your key components of success in India is what makes you successful at home.

Do not underestimate the cost of understanding and documenting what you do and what you apparently already know. The cost of developing an up to date house manual — for this is what is required — can often be a hidden cost to companies. On the other hand, not developing your house manual will cause you much greater costs and although they will be hidden from you at the start of business development in India, you will not be able to hide them from anyone once they start to mount.

You may even find that this cost, whether you allowed for it or not, turns into a hidden benefit in due course as you start to examine your home functions critically as a result of developing the house manual.

Hidden Benefits

In my experience, the major hidden benefit of entering the Indian domestic market is that it provides a platform for a number of successive hidden benefits. The speed with which a new operation can be brought into serious profitability can be astonishing. That speed means that the return on your investment can kick in faster than you might imagine. At the same time, you will be engaged with a new work force which will look at your company and the way it goes to market with entirely fresh eyes.

If you make a survey of companies that have entered the Indian market, asking them how long before their new business was cash positive, you will get a range of answers, and sometimes a range of answers from the same company about one project. The truth is that this is of course commercially extremely sensitive, and, more importantly, internally politically sensitive. As a prudent business planner, it is wise to suggest that from the moment your business development project starts in India, you should allow a minimum of twenty four months to become cash positive and another six to eight months before you will be profitable.

Many of the companies that I have dealt with or asked directly have told me that these figures are about right. Of course there are huge variations — often smoothed or glossed, not by the real world but by corporate expectations that starting a new business just does take that amount of time before it will be cash positive and the fact that knowing when a company is actually profitable is such a black art that it is difficult to tell. The view that I have built up of new entrants into India is that, despite the price sensitivity that is endemic in Indian business life across nearly all domains, there is real sense in planning your next metro as soon as you have commenced trading in your first so that you are ready to spin into action as soon as you have enough cash or as soon as you know that you are going to be cash positive very soon.

Yet that hidden benefit of what should be a relatively fast return on investment is dwarfed by another that is enabled by it. Taking six months from first trading as the time that will elapse before you have a functioning centre, it will take another six to twelve months to become a mature business environment. During that transition you will discover that fresh, well educated and intelligent eyes, initially a hidden cost because of their inexperience, will become a hidden then overt benefit as they will look closely at all aspects of your business and will start to make subtle, and then probably more dramatic, improvements. Of course I have seen this benefit snuffed out by an insecure expatriate manager, but if you have chosen your senior manager carefully, one who values flexibility and openness to change, you will surprise yourself with the difference your Indian operation can make to your home company — if you let it.

You will possibly find that any data produced by your company is being analysed in unexpected ways, and these will reveal cost cutting opportunities that you hadn't contemplated. You will have suggestions about making your processes faster and less complicated and a bewilderment at what you consider to be normal. All suggestions and ideas will not necessarily be sensible or positive, but even having your ideas challenged will be valuable. I have been surprised that this benefit can remain hidden for so long in some companies which do not realise what is happening and how new ideas are enlivening what they do.

In short, you will be examining what you do and how you do it in greater detail than you would normally apply to your usual business processes, but with the benefit of fewer presuppositions and more disinterested analysts. Your Indian staff will be trained in your processes but they will still be new to them. This might be a wasting benefit, but properly handled it would not be.

The next hidden benefit of entering the Indian market is closely related to the one above, as entering the Indian market can have a direct impact on your company's way of developing strategy. You will find that not only do your Indian staff start to push you in unexpected directions, creating a different perspective on strategy, but you will be able to experiment with ideas and marketing initiatives in the Indian market at much less cost than at home.

When I discuss recruitment, in Chapter 10, you will see my emphasis on being open minded about any limited previous experience amongst your candidates. This is where the undoubted extra cost of training is more than balanced by the freshness, academic achievement and intelligence of your recruits.

One of the significant hidden benefits is the quality of the people that you will be recruiting. Where you would not be able to consider a graduate in the West, you will naturally appoint graduates. They will be highly motivated not just to do a good job but to make a success of your company. It is a hidden benefit because very often companies do not even directly realise how much difference their new Indian employees are making to their company by just bringing a different, engaging and challenging capability to what they do. There may be many moments when cultural differences with your staff will make you wonder why you attempted to take on India, but overall you will know why when you consider the asset Indian staff can be.

These benefits, hidden and totally submerged in some cases, are significant enough, but when they are seen in the round and combined with another aspect of Indian corporate life they become really significant.

Modern western corporations have taken to trumpeting their flexibility and fleetness of foot when addressing new markets. As with any brave claim this often disguises just the opposite. Anyone who has much experience of western corporate life knows how long it takes to push a new idea to the point where it even achieves visibility, let alone implementation, in a mature corporate environment.

Your Indian business, once it is mature enough to take on something of a life of its own, will be very different. If you watch Indian business people as closely as I do, your respect will grow and grow. This is not just because you will be watching an extremely successful group of people. You will probably soon become aware of a quality that will be initially alarming and then amazingly important. For a number of reasons, not least the importance of the trader and the entrepreneur in Indian business, Indian companies are remarkably flexible. And they change as quickly as circumstances change.

For a start they watch each other like hawks and any discussion with an Indian business person who analyses the competition will show you insights that are generally profound and always thought provoking, even if they are odd. Indian managers watch their markets closely and respond to changes very quickly indeed. As I have discussed above, they also monitor what is going on in the West and western business with a degree of attention that you will find surprising.

If you in turn watch your Indian managers and staff carefully and discuss trends and market changes with them, you will have a lightning rod into market development both in India and in your domestic market. In addition, watching how India Inc or India Ltd responds to western markets will give you insights into your domestic market in a way that only very expensive research will approach. You will have an insight into what your domestic competition is about to engage in very early in your competitor's planning cycle.

I have come to regard this very much hidden benefit as particularly significant, and likely to become more important over time. One of my clients said to me, some nine months into developing his business offshore, that I had promised that his domestic business would be revitalised by entering the Indian market. He had doubted it, but had come to realise in a very short time that this was undoubtedly true. Of course you have to be open to new ideas and able to withstand the shocks of getting into India, but if you do, the hidden benefits will repay the effort.

Then there is a benefit that I cannot usually say is hidden very much, but which becomes buried as you start analysing whether you want to go to India and how to do it. The actual cost of getting into the market is still very low. You will be paying intelligent, albeit inexperienced graduates some $600 or £300 per month. And even if wage inflation doubles that, you will still be gaining an enormous benefit at rates below your own market.

This leads me full circle back to the issues with your procurement department and gives another reason why you should approach going into the Indian market with a keen awareness of the differences involved. If you select suppliers that appear to be geared up to your needs because they know how to mimic what you are used to but they are really some sort of pragmatic hybrid, you may well lose this aspect of working with India as a benefit. If you work with an Indian company that can actually understand your requirements but still retain its distinctive Indian qualities, its value to you will be that much more, even if in the short term it is more difficult to work together or it is uncomfortable for the procurement department.

Finally

Over the years I have been getting underneath the range of hidden costs first in going offshore and then getting into the Indian market, and then analysing the hidden benefits. Because of that experience and because of the way that Indian business is maturing, it is becoming easier to see how to turn what are initially hidden costs into hidden and then overt benefits. This process will speed up and as the business world becomes more homogenised I expect that some of the benefits from cross-fertilisation will weaken. Yet there is still an excitement in this environment that means that every business person has to be aware of the hidden benefits and the hidden costs — and know how to deal with both sides of the equation.

To make a success of entering the Indian market, you will have to be very rigorous in challenging your normal assumptions. If you do so properly, you will find that there is a hidden cost even here, and one that is difficult to quantify, as it may largely result in lost time. Yet I am convinced that not long after you have absorbed this hidden cost, you will start to find that it has enormous hidden benefits, not just in your current project, but in encouraging you to take the same approach to all your business issues.

T W O

WHY INDIA?

Every time that I discuss entering the Indian domestic market, I am asked why India — and why now? These are the key questions and should be uppermost in your mind as you consider whether to enter the Indian market now or at all.

As I have briefly mentioned, there are good economic reasons, not least the growth rate, the disposable incomes, the burgeoning middle class, and the appetite in India for western goods and services. Yet you can look elsewhere and find other countries that offer similar — if not better — apparent reasons for considering them. We always encourage our clients to put India in a proper economic perspective and it is also worth looking briefly at some of the other areas to be considered.

The analysis here is not comprehensive but indicative. It does not make sense for every company — and we work with our clients on an individual basis that is not possible here. One client came back to me after considering all the arguments and said that actually the answer was the Philippines.

And my question about how much the civil war there would affect the prospects was shrugged aside.

China is the obvious competitor. And the best way of making your Indian embassy or high commission act is to mention China casually as being under consideration. There is not much else that makes them responsive but this can have a real effect and even make them think about doing something.

China has an economy growing faster than India's 11% plus as opposed to 9%. It is in manufacturing in a way that India is only just beginning to do more than dream about. It has a balance of trade for the twelve months to July 2007 of 229 billion dollars, compared with India's imbalance of 63 billion dollars. Industrial production in the same period was up more than 18%, compared with India's 12.5%. The Indian figure is by no means scanty — but China's production is growing 50% faster. Consumer prices are growing at about 3.5% whereas in India they are growing by over 6%. Its stock market prices have grown at about 40% and in dollar terms by about 90% in a year, compared with India's stock price change of 8% and 18% respectively.

It must be doing quite a lot right, too, because foreign direct investment into China is running at nearly 42 billion dollars. The increase year on year is about 18%. There are fluctuations in the figures, but whichever way you look at it, it is substantial. This compares with India which *only* attracted 16 billion dollars, although this was up more than three times on the previous year when it was some five billion dollars. These are obviously snap shots and are not particularly reliable figures taken on their own — there are times when the UK, for example, tops the league table when one of its major corporations is taken over.

For sometimes simplistic reasons, and sometimes because of their loose but increasingly effective alliance on various issues, such as agricultural pricing, China and India are lumped with two other rapidly developing countries into an acronym and known as the BRICs. The other two members of the BRIC group of countries, Russia and Brazil, are also worthy of consideration.

Brazil is growing at a respectable 4.3%, more than twice as fast as the US and more than a third faster than the Euro area. Industrial production is up by nearly 5% year on year. It has a positive trade balance of 47 billion dollars. Inflation is around 3.7% at consumer price level. Its stock market has increased in value by more than 26% — and more than 42% in dollar terms.

Similarly Russia has a positive trade balance of over 128 billion dollars, an economy growing at nearly 8%, industrial production growing at more than 6% and inflation at more than 8%. With its huge energy reserves that are really only just coming on tap, Russia's willingness to use its strength in the market to grow its revenues, and an increasingly friendlier attitude towards foreign direct investment, there is obviously a case to consider Russia seriously. It might just be the gas station to the world, but it is some gas station.

Another area that I encourage my clients to look at is what used to be known as Eastern Europe — the new members of the European Union. Hungary's industrial production is growing at 6% per annum. The Czech Republic is growing at 14%. The competitive landscape, however, and the proximity to western Europe and wage inflation is the key major issue there.

Similarly the Gulf is certainly awash with money and growth, with Dubai, especially, looking an attractive market — and it currently has the largest percentage of the world's cranes supporting its property development.

Singapore with an 18% increase in industrial production and an 8% growth rate is another candidate — and in that sense the list, particularly in Asia, is endless.

Against that, I still say that the answer to *why India* is probably *why not?* The economic reasons for going to India are there, but India has special advantages that are, of course, related to the economic background, but which are extraordinarily powerful. Rather than comparing India with other countries, which would take forever, I will address the reasons why India has to be considered.

In my experience with clients, there is initially some resistance to the criteria I use. But having worked in the Gulf and discussed at great length these issues with people whose main focus is China, I am confident that they produce an argument that has to be taken notice of.

I start with what some of my clients initially view as rather soft issues. India is a democracy. It is a vibrant democracy too. In fact the Indian launch of my previous book on India was made much more problematic by the results of the general election in 2004, when the electorate, despite the booming economy and the ruling coalition's slogan, *India shining!*, threw the rascals out and installed a completely different coalition, albeit one headed by the man who had started the fiscal, economic and regulatory revolution in India, Manmohan Singh.

India's democracy is proof that while politicians may rarely leave the public stage other than rich — for reasons that are well documented — they do leave the political stage there against their will.

India has a free press. And it is extraordinarily free and refreshingly outspoken too. That independence in the press is really vital. Having worked in countries where the press is controlled by the government and seen how facts are completely mishandled and where no one can be held to account, made me appreciate the press in India more and more. No one is beyond criticism in the Indian papers any more than they are in the West. There is bias. There is sensationalism. There is a focus on the trivial. Yet there is also an engagement with the issues and some real fearlessness in the press.

Even Bollywood stars are criticised. In any developing country like India where the vector between the educated and powerful and the poorly educated and weak is enormous, this feature of the country is vital. I well remember my manager in Delhi hectoring a policeman — he called him a cop — for having the temerity to stop him for speeding. It was clearly apparent that the policeman did not know how important my manager was and the sheer confidence with which he was dressed down, ensured that he eventually gave an apology for having stopped us. In this type of society this relatively minor abuse of position can be reproduced at higher and higher levels — so that, for example, individuals appear to be above the law. Drunken Bollywood stars have killed innocent poor people asleep on the pavement — and could get away with it, were it not for the free press. The potential for exposure is always there, and this acts as a fine restraint in many areas of business.

Similarly there is a rule of law in India. The law basis is common law — which makes it easy for the UK and US to understand it — and, while it has diverged over the last sixty years from the UK legal structures that spawned it, the threads remain visible and active. The law is there and it is, eventually, effective.

Of course it is grindingly slow. If you think it takes a long time to set up a company in India — and it does — winding one up takes forever. One of my business acquaintances had been trying to wind up a partnership perfectly amicably for over eight years. The processes are labyrinthine if that is not unfair to the home of the Minotaur. Yet this is changing — and changing reasonably fast.

As pressures on retention of staff have built up in certain hot spots in India, such as Bangalore and Chennai, companies have resorted to imposing contractual obligations on staff. One company that I have worked with that is mainly focused on services to publishers in the scientific and academic worlds, early recognised that almost the most they could expect from a new graduate was about 30 months service before they would be tempted into higher paid jobs that were not quite so tedious. With that sort of time frame they could maintain continuity and by recruiting new graduates keep their employment costs down. This parallels the economic model of many off-shoring companies which is based on attrition and continuously recruiting lower paid staff.

On the other hand, this model does require a certain period of service and continuity to make it work. When the period of service that they could rely on was reduced to less than a year, things were rather desperate, particularly as training took at least three months and a handover took a month. They resorted to a contract with each new recruit which imposed penalties if the person left before two years was up. By building the cost of the employee's induction, training and other benefits into the contract they came up with a sensible figure that would be regarded by a court as justifiable and the contract with the employee sugessted that this would be repaid if the employee left before completing the contracted period of time. The focus on a cost is important as rules aganist restraint of trade mean that no employee can be bound to work for a period of time.

The obligation was lightly regarded by the new employees who thought they knew that the courts would take forever to make a decision and it would be more expensive for the company to sue them than to let them go. By hiring the best barrister, creating the greatest amount of presence through the press and other public relations activities, and pursuing the issues as hard as possible, the company got judgement against the employees who had left within six months.

This astonished the employees — and astonished the court officials almost as much — but it had the right effect. While the employees who had been sued were more or less written off, not one employee has since tested the validity of the contract — and the economic model of the company has survived and it goes from strength to strength.

This will not happen every time — and make no mistake the court process will try the patience of a devil let alone a saint — but it is an indication that the rule of law in the company arena is not only a capable, but can be a useful, ally.

The fourth area in this group is the regulatory framework that exists in India. This is more often than not associated with two rather unpleasant side effects. The first is that India is known for its stifling regulatory regime. The whole economy used to be characterised as the Licence Raj. Sometimes you can feel it in the very air as you discuss with a bureaucrat why it is that your perfectly reasonable request for permission to add something to the articles of your company is impossible to achieve during this lifetime. (Being a Hindu does give certain advantages, because, of course, it does mean that you have at least a second life in which to achieve this impossibility.)

The breadth and scope of business regulations in India means that it is almost impossible to anticipate the actual hurdle that you will face.

It is useful here to know about stamped paper which is essential to the agreement of most serious contractual activities. This you have to buy and then print your agreement on it — you cannot add the stamp later. It also has a shelf life — so you usually cannot buy it in advance. With time ticking away — imperceptibly slowly though it may seem — while you negotiate with a potential client, do keep an eye on the clock and give yourself time to buy the stamped paper if there is a contract involved.

The second side effect is that, of course, this being India, if there is a hurdle, there is usually a way round it rather than over it. Factory inspections used to be notorious as a means of not exactly enriching but still rewarding factory inspectors whose eyesight could be remarkably influenced by small amounts of money and whose subsequent judgements could be certainly biased against the facts. This has led to serious abuses in India over the years, especially in the field of child labour which is a continuing scandal in some states.

On the other hand, there is now a more positive aspect to business regulation in India. Inspection regimes are being tightened up and some of the larger scandals that have been exposed in the newspapers have meant that there is a new honesty and a new determination about enforcing regulations in a positive way. Of course if you queue for a visa or to have permission for a company start up in your local embassy or high commission, having already obtained the necessary apostille, you may feel there is a long way to go. (The very fact of needing an apostille, though it is quite an engaging word to learn, is also part of this education.) The penetration of the formal or organised economy in India, that is the economy that is properly part of the regulatory and fiscal environment, by effective health and safety legislation and other regulatory instruments is something that is now understood by Indian business people to be a key to India's growth in the global economy. To continue to thrive on the world stage India needs to ensure that it is relatively clean in terms of factory, shop and office health and safety.

As regulations become enforced in a less arbitrary way, there are opportunities for western companies to enter the Indian market.

These four areas, democracy, rule of law, the free press and an effective and sensible regulatory environment, make a huge difference to doing business in India compared with some of the non-democratic countries with their controlled press and virtually unregulated local officials. India is not perfect in any of these areas, but it is recognisably moving in the right direction from an increasingly reasonable base.

The infrastructure issues, partly dealt with in the previous chapter, are two edged, as we have seen. There are real issues with electricity and power supply, with logistics, with transport and with construction generally. Yet the scale of the requirements and the commitment to removing the barriers to infrastructure development are so strong, that this is a really positive indicator for India. By no means is India in a good position as far as its business infrastructure is concerned, but it is changing relatively quickly and the awareness of the need for change is highly important.

Another extremely positive reason for considering India is the demographic profile of the country. By various estimates — and I never actually trust a figure in India, just the trend — more than half the population is under the age of 25. This is still a genuinely growing population. Compare that with China where the number of people of working age goes into decline from about 2015, where Russia is already in quite a steep decline, and contrast that with the whole European Union where, despite the recent new entrants, there is forecast to be a shortfall of about 11 million in the working age population by the same date, and you can see how significant a consumer market India will be.

On current trends, however, this apparently positive profile has a negative side, in that there will be a surplus of about 47 million people in India of working age by about 2020. If these are poor people, as that would suggest, then the internal market in India starts to look very troubled. If you couple that with political unrest that exists anyway and social unrest caused by the unequal distribution of the rewards from India being part of the global economy, there are some storm cones to be hoisted. Political unrest is visible in India and not just in Kashmir and Jammu, but in Assam and even in Andhra Pradesh, where the Chief Minister has five white Ambassador cars with the same registration plate so that an assassin would not necessarily know which one he occupies.

This is where international comparisons are very difficult. It is fair enough to suggest that the old Eastern Europe will be quite stable, though the emigration of a sizeable percentage of the brightest and best amongst the twenty somethings is causing some havoc to economic projections. Yet knowing what is going on in China is almost impossible to fathom and Russia is impenetrable, if not to the same extent. It is probably fair to say that the political stability of Russia cannot be taken for granted.

It is important to recognise at the same time that there are real reasons why the political stability of India may be under extreme pressure. I do not see this as a red light to stop consideration of India, but there is certainly an amber warning here and it is as well to choose where you will establish your company with some care.

The issues over demographics and political unrest have a bearing and direct influence on two other important areas to be considered when analysing which country's market to enter. These are education and the use of English.

Education in India is the field in which almost the biggest contrasts exist. At the ordinary state school level, the education provided is patchy and unreliable. It is often said that it is either the students or the teachers who are not bothering to turn up — and where you have teachers you have no students and where you have students you have no teachers. Some states do much better than others and at a national and a state level there are serious efforts being made to improve education provision, but there is a steep hill to climb.

The situation can be so difficult that extraordinary developments have taken place in pockets round the country. In Hyderabad, for example, there are many private schools which serve the poorer communities. The parents make enormous sacrifices to pay upwards from as little as five rupees a day for their children to be educated in English in private schools. When I was told about them by a UK educational trust that asked me to help it establish in Hyderabad, I could hardly believe that such schools existed. Not only do they exist but they are in federations. The educational trust, CfBT, is there to support the schools professionally and if you want to see dedication to education and belief in the future, just go to the schools. You do not have to be as emotional as I am to be deeply affected.

For students that multi-national companies will be interested in employing, the education is world class. Not all the two million or so graduates per year will be of global quality, but the standard coming out of the Indian Institutes of Management (IIMs) and the Indian Institutes of Technology (IITs) will be very high.

Between those two extremes there is a large, developing middle class who speak English. It is a different English in many ways but it is English and it is a common language through the country. This gives India an enormous edge in global business — and it also makes it a good deal easier for foreign companies entering the Indian market. The constitution recognises 22 official languages, with English recognised as a co-official language. With this plethora of languages it can be a good party trick to know that Marathi is the official language of Maharastra and Telegu the official language for Andhra Pradesh. In practice, the customer base that a foreign entrant will probably be targeting will have scarcely an issue using English as the medium of marketing and sales, let alone internal discussion.

It is a different English — the words may not mean quite what you expect. In the UK, for example, the word "rascal" has connotations of naughty or some form of rather innocent roguery. When reading an article in *The Times of India* on my first trip you can imagine my surprise to see that a band of men who had robbed and killed a couple were described as "rascals".

The accent will be different in India, but as I always point out probably no more impenetrable than some of the regional variations within the UK and the US.

I take the easy use of English as a very significant element in choosing to go to India as a market.

On the other hand, use of European languages other than English is very restricted. You will still find pockets of Portuguese around Goa, which was part of the Portuguese empire until the sixties, and French in and around Pondicherry, now known by some as Puducherry, which was French until 1956. Beyond that, India has had very limited exposure to European languages. Of course this is not so much an issue if you are entering the market, as you can use the global business language, English.

The next factor is one that affects business process offshoring immediately and only secondarily those companies setting up in India, but it can be insidiously significant. There is a lack of western business domain skills in India because business is generally conducted in quite a different way. Essentially, as one example, India still has a second world banking infrastructure set inside a third world cost environment — as compared with, say, South Africa, where banking and insurance are very recognisable in western terms. This lack of knowledge of how business is properly conducted in the West generally becomes important to the market entrant some time after first entering the market when what you might take for granted is not at all the local expectation.

When working in South Africa, it is very easy to pick up how business is conducted but in India it is difficult, although the superficial appearance may give a different impression. In my experience this lack of knowledge in India means that the entrant has to work doubly hard to understand and be understood. Accounts, invoicing, orders and other general administration matters are common across business cultures and can lull the unsuspecting into a false sense of security. For example, payments and how they are handled and prioritised are another matter. In discussing the various countries that could be targets for market entry, India will not come out as a first choice necessarily using this criterion. The saving factor is that you will soon learn.

Quality awareness is very high in India, particularly in the service industries and if your company has a high regard for quality, then India is a congenial place to set up. This is, of course, a generalisation and you will find examples of the lowest possible awareness of quality. More significant than any variation in quality is what is meant by quality. At a very high level it is possible to characterise the difference between the western view of quality and the Indian view as the difference between focusing on the end result and focusing on the process. The results may be very similar, but the different perspective can be very telling.

In the West quality means a wide variety of things, but it is essentially looking at fitness for purpose and getting something right first time. Quality is not so much in how the product or service was produced but in how it was finally perceived by the customer. In India, the concentration is on the process and getting that right during the production, preparation or delivery of a service. If you follow the prescribed steps, the result must be high quality, against a western view which is really only concerned with the finished article.

The real difference for a foreigner trying to work in India is in the mutual incomprehension about what quality means. You might think this is relatively trivial, but it can cause a fair amount of pain.

Nevertheless, it is still an environment where a quality perspective is understood and appreciated, and this makes India a suitable environment for the quality focused company.

Service excellence is a different kettle of fish. What my Indian friends and colleagues regard as assertiveness — and which can look very much like aggression to me — is much more common when dealing with clients and customers than the way we expect to interact in the West. This is probably an uncomfortable area to learn about and experience at first hand but not one that needs to detain us too much. It just takes a bit of adjusting to. I know that when I first watched my Indian sales people in India dealing with clients I was baffled and rather alarmed. It is quite a significant difference.

Throughout this book, there will be references to the bureaucracy that can seem to dominate Indian business life. It is all pervasive and inescapable and will drive you mad. Having worked and managed businesses in the Gulf

I have to say it does not really hold a candle to what Oman and the UAE officialdom can do to you, but in western terms it is an eye opener.

There is a new positive aspect to the bureaucracy that, partly because it is India, has an inevitable downside. Many bureaucratic functions in India are being outsourced to the private sector — although some of the major conglomerates that are being given the work look and feel like extensions of the Indian Administrative Service in any case.

The upside is that there is a service ethos — of sorts — and there is more sense of something happening. (I have been in bureaucrats' offices where the movement of the hour hand on the clock on the wall seemed hurried by comparison.) The downside is that in the past, minor issues or slight mistakes in the paperwork could be solved by the bureaucrat using his or her discretion, aided by a small exchange of money. Nowadays it is back to square one and starting again, even if it means having all the documents notarised again in the home country. The Indian expressive shrug has a new meaning when that is the message.

In real terms, apart from the times when you will be slowed to a crawl by some official demand, the environment is not that intrusive in the normal run of business.

The ante-penultimate item to be considered when assessing whether India is the best target country for your presence is time zones. India, being 4.5 to 5.5 hours ahead of the UK and 9.5 to 13.5 hours ahead of the US, has advantages and disadvantages. If you want a report on your desk first thing your time about yesterday's trading it is excellent. If you need to exercise close control of processes it can be an issue. Planning is the answer as it is to most business issues.

I always ask clients to consider what impact time zones might have once they have a business running in India, but the truth is that the issue is not usually a show stopper.

The penultimate item is the one that I develop a little more below. If you have already taken work offshore, it is very likely you will have at least considered India as a destination market. Even if you finally made the decision not to put work offshore, there may well be some research that backed up your decision not to go. This means that somewhere within your organisation there is a body of knowledge about India and the way business is conducted. This does make India easier to consider as a target market, and while companies very often have not quite realised what in-house information they already have, when they are reminded it does provide a platform for further consideration.

When I am asked to compare India with the other BRIC countries using these criteria, it is usually a simple process to eliminate the other countries. Clearly this means my criteria are skewed but not, I believe, by India. It is the result of many years of experience during which time these criteria have been found to have value.

Finally there is corruption. I deal with this elsewhere, but do keep it in mind. I have been engaged to sort out too many frauds offshore not to take this very seriously, and there is no substitute for being both sceptical and wary. In my experience it is not as bad in India as it is elsewhere, but it is not something to be dismissed. I am not referring to the relatively low level of bribes — to get a document through the bureaucracy for example — but to large scale bribes and fraud which do occur.

The real question then is not why India, but why not — and even so I do not want to paint too rosy a picture. Getting into India is fraught and penetrating the market is fraught. Yet no more so than most other non-western countries.

In my view if the answer to the question is why not, then there are a number of steps that most businesses should be thinking through now. Most western businesses will at least have considered taking aspects of their IT systems offshore, whether its development or the complete running of their systems. There are some reasons why you would not have done that, but not many that stand any real test, which is a proper analysis of costs and benefits. Many businesses have considered taking their normal administration offshore, and increasingly this is seen as a low risk, high reward strategy. While once the preserve only of larger companies with a small army of administrators in Gurgaon or Chennai, now companies can have even as few as one, two or three administrators in India, looking after anything from customer records through to overall financial administration.

All companies looking to expand their market should now be considering India — as you will see from this book. If you have not already gone offshore for IT or business services, you should be considering doing so. If you have already taken at least some steps in that direction, you have a stepping stone to entering the Indian domestic market. Any supplier you have engaged will be well placed to help you understand the issues and the first steps and help you understand the various perspectives you will need in order to set up in India. The health warning is that your supplier will probably be quite limited — his or her focus will be on the export market from India — you.

If you have not already used offshore services, you are at a small disadvantage of course, but, as I have seen with clients, it need not be a great disadvantage. The paradox is that a small acquaintance with India can very quickly give the impression that you understand it, and some companies that are already using offshore services have the impression that they know rather more, and, even worse, understand rather more than they actually do about India and Indian business. They will, for example, have chosen their supplier on a number of criteria, not all of which will actually stand scrutiny — and the supplier will inevitably be more westernised in approach than the Indian business people you will have to deal with in India itself.

The point is to use all sources of information you can and start with any knowledge that lies inside your company already as the path to understanding what is happening in India, where it is happening, and whether this is of direct interest to you.

If it is of interest, then the serious work has to start finding out what the pitfalls are.

It is difficult to enter the Indian market and this is why we as a consultancy make money. It is business planning against a mountain of uncertainty. What we find, when we are taking people and companies through the stages, is that there is an uncomfortable feeling in our audience that they actually already *know* what we are talking about, but we think that it is more that they recognise the truth in what we are saying.

The real issue is around what is missing in India that you have come to take for granted in your home market. If you set up a business in the West, you can rely on other companies to provide you with the services you need. Whether it is fast logistics or good IT service, whether it is installation of Internet links at the drop of a hat or company registration that can be done over the Net, in India it can usually be a major obstacle to progress just when you least expect it.

Everything in India takes time — more time that you will allow no matter how experienced you are.

What I keep up my sleeve for all the times companies look at me and say that this is taking longer than we expected — though most have the grace to concede eventually that it is as long as we told them to anticipate — is the real silver lining to what is admittedly a particularly black cumulo nimbus. Do keep in mind that if you find it difficult to deal with market entry in India, imagine what a barrier to entry this is to those companies that will follow you. Indeed the major hurdle to being successful in India is the sheer complexity of getting through the glass walls and once you have done so you have a major advantage over any competitors trying to follow you.

My best example is from setting up my first company in India years ago. The company that I was working for had been refused permission to set up in India on what I thought were extraordinarily good grounds. (Just when you expect India to be irrational and obstructive, it will turn on you and be rational and obstructive.) My task was to guide the company through this serious objection — from the Reserve Bank of India, no less. Using my network as opposed to trying to question the various officials who seemed to have perfected the dismissive shrug years before I got to them, I discovered that the only way forward was to create a not-for-profit company. What the government's chief financial institution disliked was the idea that a foreign educational trust was attempting apparently to make money out of educational services aimed at relatively poor people. (As I say, I thought this entirely reasonable.) They were very happy to allow foreign direct investment, but not to make money out of extraordinarily poor people.

Accepting this, everything went swimmingly, and by the mere expedient of flying to Delhi and virtually camping in the overflowing office — overflowing with paper, humanity and shrugs — I managed to get the various paper stages covered. Of course, the next stage was obtaining foreign direct investment permission. As a commercial company, permission for foreign direct investment had been forthcoming, but the company was not allowed to be a commercial one. As a non-commercial company, however, foreign direct investment was a different matter. This seemed like an impasse.

The rationale for the objection is long-seated in India and soundly based. In the early days of philanthropy towards India, all sorts of charitable trusts set up in India and built extraordinarily expensive facilities and gave them to India. This left the Indians with clinics, colleges and hospitals which were marvellous but unaffordable. As a result, India started to become very picky about non-profit making foreign direct investment in India.

The argument for blocking the foreign direct investment made sense in each of its stages, but as a whole it sort of fell to pieces. The damning final position was that the foreign direct investment to set up the educational trust would not make a profit — especially as it was not allowed to as it had to be set up as a non-profit making organisation.

If the company did not make a profit, it was clearly unsustainable and would be just like the gargantuan early examples of philanthropy and so it should not be given permission to invest. It would be allowed if it could make a profit because that would prove it was not what one official told me with a completely straight face — a white elephant. On the other hand, no UK educational trust would be allowed to set up a profit making offshoot in India, as that was unethical.

It took six months and extreme ingenuity to get round that little setback. The answer was not to tackle the root problem but to go round it in time honoured Indian fashion. If the money coming in was not treated as investment, it was fine. It was treated as payment for services.

The UK's accountants were never actually convinced that this was acceptable, which shows how unimaginative accountants can be. The argument that drew their fangs was when I asked them whether anyone would pay for services it was not getting. No accountant could imagine that, so the accounts were passed.

My proposition is to get there and establish your company. You will then find that everyone else will find it extraordinarily difficult to establish their companies in India — giving you a significant amount of first mover advantage.

You may find you pay for a few services you will be hard pressed to point to — but the miracle will be that you will be established and can trade.

THREE

UNDERSTANDING INDIANS AND INDIAN BUSINESS

Y ou will find that for every generalisation about India there are more generalisations that disprove what you are saying. Nonetheless, I have to start with a major generalisation that I have found more useful than not over the years.

The main fact about Indian business is that what underlies Indian business, and has been there for all the years that the Portuguese — who were there first from Europe, and the French — who were there before and after the Brits, and the Brits who were there in the most substantial form — is the fact that it is, above all else, a trading nation. Indian business is essentially trading. There are manufacturers, there are developers, there are entrepreneurs, there are crooks, and there are bureaucrats, but at heart everyone of them in my experience is a trader. Whether there is value add or not, I have found that the best approach to an Indian business person is to imagine that he or she wants to sell you something, and if that something is not yet in his or her possession, so much the better.

As a salesman in the UK, Europe and the US, I have dealt with financiers, who understand finance, insurers who understand insurance, hoteliers who understand hospitality and professionals who understand fees. In India it is useful to know these domains, but it is far better to understand that what underpins Indian business is selling something.

Having dealt with Indians in many different market places, and met some who do not conform to the picture that I am painting, I know that this is the most valuable insight you can have into the Indian business psyche.

In the West I have met consummate sales people. One, especially — Martin Palmer — worked with me in the nineties and turned every conversation into a sales process. When his wife asked him what he wanted for dinner, he would ask, completely unconsciously, why she was asking that question. (As a salesman, he never answered a question from a potential customer with anything but a question — it was an opportunity to find out more about the customer and the particular requirements. He did not know he did it. He just did it. You can imagine what negotiating with him was like.) Martin is an exceptional salesman even amongst western sales people. In India he would be one of the best but still one of many.

I am convinced that Indians feel the way a market is developing and can detect subtle changes in demand without even actually consciously noticing it. They change direction without blinking, whereas a typical western corporation will still be working out the next twelve month's budget and sales projections.

This is disconcerting and I have known various western business people who have been completely thrown by the experience of dealing with an Indian business person for the first time. With this perspective in mind, it can be a great deal easier to understand Indian business and Indian business methods.

There is little in India that smacks of a sentimental devotion to the past. I came to the conclusion very soon that this was a paradoxical aspect of having so much past all around them every day. India is littered with reminders of waves of invaders, different cultures, different religions, and different perspectives and treats them with scant regard. Similarly, a company that has grown fast on one series of products or services, can quite readily abandon it and become an entirely different company.

44

There is an *as well as* culture of course — and you only have to look at the big conglomerations, such as the Tata empire and the Reliance empire to see that, yet even these reveal the same way of doing business. Each of them, for example, is in mobile telephones because they were looking for the next big market and when they entered the mobile phone market this was going to be it. Demand is what drives the Indian market — which is a truism and yet it seems quite different from western markets. Indian companies are always looking for the next big area and scenting the way the market is going. It is a highly responsive market and while innovation is beginning to happen in certain industries, such as pharmaceuticals, it is best to see it in those terms as I discuss later when considering how to go to market in India.

The biggest contrast is with Silicon Valley where demand is created rather than responded to. That is an imperfect statement too, but clients have found it a useful guideline. I do not want to push the contrast too hard. You will inevitably find Indian businesses that are at the cutting edge of fashion, demand creation, technology and ideas, just the same as you will find American corporations that are expert at being highly successful second movers, eliminating the initial company in the field. Yet it is always the contrast that is important to understand and the different perspective and this is what is most instructive about Indian business.

If you think of Indian business as highly sensitive to the way a market, indeed the whole market, is moving — they are as quick to get out of a market as they are to get in — and driven by traders and a trading mentality, you will have a good basis for understanding the Indian domestic market and how best to penetrate it.

The danger for a company coming into the market and looking for initial customers is, of course, the opposite of the usual western experience and I have found many disappointed western business people, frustrated by the corollary of this very readiness to pick up new ideas and approaches.

As opposed to the usual western experience of having to create business plans and cases in infinite detail and hawking this round external suppliers or trying to create interest internally in the company, Indians will welcome new ideas and new approaches with open arms. For those of us in the West long enough in business to have attempted to develop opportunities, creating the audience is the first and often extremely tedious process in business development. It will not be a pushover in India, but you will find an audience reasonably quickly, and it will be receptive and even moderately enthusiastic very quickly.

The problem is that there is always someone else behind you with another exciting idea that is already breaking fast in western markets. The rapidity with which you will be welcomed by an Indian business person will be matched by the, often uncommunicated, speed with which interest will wane and the next big idea will be adopted.

It only becomes an issue if you are not prepared for this, but, of course, it is the other side of the same coin. I do not think that Indians are more fickle but their business processes are so much faster than western norms, you may get caught out.

Short termism is something that major corporations acknowledge throughout the world, especially in the US, where quarterly reporting focuses the average CXO's mind very often on the next three months if not the next week. In India it is different. It is a sense of the future that I personally find exhilarating but which can also be daunting. The Indian mindset is not to ditch something because it takes a long time to give a return. The Indian mindset is to attach itself to the next big thing and in that process what was there before may inevitably get squeezed out. This is not any more of a problem than any comparable issue in the West. As long as you can keep that perspective in your mind, you will be safe.

There is another driver that I have alluded to often in these pages, but it is one that permeates the consciousness of every globally minded Indian business person, which is a huge percentage of the business people you will encounter. It is China.

China is many things to India. It is a role model, a competitor, a threat, an ally, an enemy, a supplier, an offshoring destination and sometimes all of these at the same time. China has been growing at 50% more than India for years largely on the back of manufacturing. India feels it has missed out and yet there is a realisation that it is not too late if the sectors are chosen carefully.

As I have said, mentioning China at strategic moments in a presentation or negotiation will often do wonders. It is a spur to action, even within the

Indian Administrative Service (IAS) — the civil service. And sometimes, as you will have seen, that takes a lot of spurs to get it moving.

Another key driver is the ambivalent feelings Indians have about their position in the world. For many justified reasons, Indians are proud of the progress they have made in the last twenty years, from a tightly controlled licence raj to a thrusting equal member of the global community. Yet there is still a very strong feeling in India that is closest to an inferiority complex. There is a need to prove themselves that seems unrealistic and unnecessary, but it does account for some strange behaviours.

This deep, pervasive attitude is atrophying, but it is slow in going. The worst example for a westerner is the need in an Indian dealing with a foreigner never to be at a loss and never to say no. It is partly politeness but it is also partly not wanting to lose face. You will find that something is always possible. In very many cases it is possible, but you can get in the ludicrous situations where you find yourself, if you have a cruel streak, seeing how far you can take this.

I have added some questions here and ask you to imagine a yes at the end of every question, and you will have it. "So we can have this through customs by the twelfth?" "You can get it delivered to the customer by the thirteenth?" You can get the money from the customer by the fourteenth?"

Even after all these years, I find it hard to deal with this aspect of the Indian business psyche, as it is all too easy to lull myself into a false sense of security hearing so much positive response and seeing them so outwardly confident.

Working with Indians is also to be tempered with one further caution related to this inability to say no.

As a chronically pessimistic business person, whose business projections exaggerate costs, downplay returns and always have massive contingency in the project plans that I produce, the Indian approach is both a breath of fresh air and an issue.

Indian business people as a group are optimistic and untrammelled by experience and by knowledge. I have, of course, met Indians who are not at all optimistic, but you should anticipate that they are always going to see the sunny side. It is like bridge players who assess a hand, and if the jack of diamonds has to sit with West, then they play the whole hand like that. Indians will, despite their own bitter trials with the government, quite naturally say to you that of course the paperwork will both be accepted by the IAS and passed by a certain date — because it has to be.

I cannot tell you that I have not been caught out by this because I have. In my early days in India, after I had been rather naive, I added 10% to any costs I was given. I added a month to the time scale. I was hopelessly out, partly, I suppose, because I wanted the costs to be right, partly because I just did not realise costs could be so different from what was stated. I had become so used to dealing with Indians that paradoxically enough I applied my normal western perspective and while I added a percentage I merely added a reasonable one.

There is no rule of thumb by the way. You cannot just double the costs you are given or just double the amount of time. Of course I do that no matter how difficult it is to persuade my western sensibility that that is what I have to do. More importantly, I still find that I have to assess the individual I am working with and start with the idea of doubling everything while being prepared to go higher. In the sense that you have to judge every individual differently it is the same as working with western suppliers or customers — it is just that much more taxing as the vector is that much wider.

It is at this point that clients usually start to think that the hurdles to entering the Indian market are too high to bother with. My perspective is that with this understanding there is a mass of opportunity to exploit. If you can understand the mindset, understand the way market opportunities are approached by Indian businesses and understand both the strengths and the shortcomings of the market, you should be in a position to make a reasoned, informed judgement whether now is the right time to enter the Indian domestic market.

In short, the questions to ask yourself are the normal ones of whether you can either complement Indian businesses or offer a competitive position that will enable you to establish your business. It is possible, of course to do both, but I find it important to pose the question in these black and white terms.

My questions are straightforward. Does strategic planning, only in its infancy in India, offer enough of an advantage that you can actually put in place a market strategy that will relentlessly allow you to get into the market in the strongest way and create a presence before anyone else notices or can respond — even taking into account the way that Indians are always looking feverishly at where markets are going?

Does second mover advantage exist in a market focused almost to the exclusion of everything else on first mover advantage and being a lightning fast follower?

By taking a realistic view of timescales and costs can you create a sounder business than the indigenous competition?

Can you provide an element of stability in a market that seems sometimes to be scrambling over itself to get to the future when the present seems to offer what you need?

In short it is essential to understand each of the peculiarities in India and the Indian market to see whether they are capable of being turned to your businessmen's advantage. I am sure that many of the issues I raise in this book seem impossible to understand and get over when they are first presented, but always keep in mind what a barrier to entry for subsequent companies that sort of feeling is.

On the other hand, I am only too aware of the other adage about working in your business taking over from working *on your* business, and it is probably true that there will be occasions when these high barriers to entry are not worth the effort of clambering over them.

The next section is one of those that will either daunt or encourage. Having gone through the pain many times, I cannot say that it actually gets any easier to bear, but it is easier to see the end of the process.

The Siege

Starting a company in India is not for the faint-hearted. If you contrast that with starting a company in the UK or the US, you will understand the scale of the issue. In the UK, for example, you can start a limited company on the Web, pay a minimal fee, and be up and running immediately with the minimal paper work following and being tidied up as you go along. I have done it many times.

Look on starting a company in India as a siege of attrition. That is really a misnomer. It is a series of sieges. You cannot actually get on a roll and once you have started winning carry on faster and faster. Each time it will be the same: a painstaking, relentless interminable drive.

There are essentially four types of company. You will have to gain several types of approval. You will need the stamped paper, of the right value, and you will need infinite patience. The documentation explaining what needs to be done is, it goes without saying, inadequate. The guidance on the value of the stamped paper that is appropriate to any document is arcane and I am convinced that there are lawyers and accountants whose only role is to estab-lish the correct value of stamped paper for any transaction. If the value is wrong, then the transaction recorded on it is not legally binding, and no amount of intention will suffice to change that fact.

Having queued as I have done in the subterranean chasm that passes for a professional, effective interface into the business life of India, the Visa Hall of the High Commission of India in the Aldwych, London, for three and a half hours, with my apostilles and my originals, my photocopies of every-thing that I could think of photocopying, and the sense that my life had already passed before my eyes, I was greeted with that patient, *I really would like to help you if only you weren't beyond assistance* look that the Indian Administrative Service clerks have perfected. The queue there is more like a raucous scrum moving imperceptibly in different directions than a serious business environment. I was told that I had not got the right number of pho-tocopies and I have to say that the first time this happened I found it quite irritating.

You will understand that I was already attuned to how that Hall works — or exists. I already knew that business document holders form part of a queue to a particular window unmarked by anything that might suggest its func-tion, alongside people who are renewing any number of strange permissions, visas, and affidavits. In fact several times during that particular lifetime on that worst of all occasions in one of the outer circles of hell I did wonder at myself for not finding it strange.

The pleasure of the occasion — I was in a queue mostly of Indians and their patience and general good humour and gallows humour jokes can keep anyone going for anything up to an hour or so of not moving anywhere in particular — was certainly undermined by the sheer noise, the claustrophobia and my increasing irritation that I was actually engaged in increasing the foreign direct investment in the country, even if only a marginal amount, and being treated effectively as a criminal.

By the time I got to the window of course, it was closing time. To his credit the clerk allowed me to run 800 yards to the nearest photocopier, and bring everything back, then he laboriously examined everything before telling me it might be ready in a day or two, and I should come back then and queue again.

I have discussed this with a High Commissioner or two and at least one Deputy High Commissioner — which role is actually responsible for this arrangement — and there is enthusiastic and ringing endorsement that this is not, perhaps, the best way of dealing with business people. It is perhaps indicative of the scale of the issue that before you enter this Hades, you have to obtain a raffle ticket to reserve a place in the queue. Being India it does no such thing, but does allow you to insist on being served that morning as the numbers on the raffle tickets are scarcely important.

This performance occurred after we had applied for the company to be set up and was only the completion of the process. I have come to the conclusion that it is quicker and less stressful to get on a plane and go to India to get the documentation sorted out.

One of the key hurdles to getting a company started in India is acquiring a Director Identification Number, or as they say in India a DIN number. For this exercise you will need to know not only your father's full name, but your paternal grandfather's full name, and have official documents with these names on and verified. (Best to use your father's birth certificate.)

It took six months in all. In India I was told it took *only* six months.

To this day, I treasure an official letter from India relating to that occurrence. Six months or so after the performance, I received a statement that my application for a "Director Identification Number (DIN) number [sic]" had been rejected for the following reason: "Handwritten DIN form/Corrections done in DIN form." This is followed by the admonition: "You are required to file a fresh application for allotment of DIN. Further you should ensure that the application is complete in all respects and the reasons for rejection as given above are fully addressed while filling the fresh application."

I have no complaints against SB Gautam, who signed the letter, reference number 90764805/763817. He is or was a Joint Director (Inspection), and is or was an Authorised Officer. How on earth could anyone file a complaint against someone who has to perform the work, as it says in the letter unsurprisingly enough, in the "DIN Processing Cell"?

I only hope that in the next life they let him work in an office because I do not bear a grudge.

The four types of companies are:

- Sole proprietorship
- A partnership
- A private limited company
- A public limited company

It is unlikely you will want to create a sole proprietorship, although there are almost no formalities in starting one. You will need any licences that are applicable to your area of trade but apart from that you can name the company, open a bank account and start trading. You, of course, have unlimited liability, and that is one of the major drawbacks.

There are reasons for establishing a partnership prior to doing anything else in India and it is a method we have used to get started relatively quickly. There has to be a partnership agreement between the various people who are involved in the business, and that will cover the usual money and legal matters, and it is sensible to get this drawn up by a lawyer in India. The only real proviso is that the business that is to be carried on has to be legal. It is also a good idea to register the partnership, although some states will not insist on that step. There is a form that is submitted along with the partnership deed to the Registrar of Firms, and that is about it, apart from the inevitable delays and the usual querying of certain aspects of the way you have filled in the forms.

There is still unlimited liability, but the formality of drawing up the partnership deed and getting the partnership registered is more satisfactory for most companies establishing themselves in India. It can also, critically, contain the exit clauses and as I will stress and stress again getting these right is your first duty. This is the case in any country, of course, but in India it is vital.

Ensure, for example, that you can go to arbitration to finish the partnership. You can go to the court, but you may find twelve years of your life disappearing as you try to unravel a partnership — and that is if you and your partners agree that you all want to end the arrangement.

We have used it successfully for clients where we wanted to have a bank account in order to start a more serious business. It allowed us to pay in funds and as soon as we started trading we could invoice and bank money.

The process for creating and registering joint stock companies is elaborate and time consuming. There are all types of companies, from non-profit companies to full blown multi-nationals, and the processes are, in general, drawn up to cater for the largest companies and smaller ones have to conform. There are many pitfalls. For any non-British readers who do not understand irony, that is an understatement.

Clearly you will not want to do this work yourself — and if you did it would almost certainly rule you out of being able to establish, register, incorporate and run a limited company as there are rules relating to lunacy and incapacity of the individuals who run companies. Nevertheless I go over the main stages below just so you know what you are missing.

All companies are governed by the Indian Companies Act of 1956, which basically set up the infrastructure, or jungle, that lawyers need to fight their way through. The act defines a company as an artificial person created by law which is a separate entity from anything else and it has, astonishingly enough, perpetuity on its side and a common seal. The latter is attached to any contract or document that the company puts forward and attests the validity of the transaction.

The legal status of such a company is broadly that of the equivalent in the West so it should not be much of a surprise. The Companies Act was really a tidying up and localising of the many companies acts that were passed during the colonial period. The usual big surprise for western companies is the degree to which the governments in India can interfere and regulate such companies, and you will find yourself sometimes subject to rather conflicting rules. At various stages in the life of the Companies Act it has been *improved* with various amendments, and some of them have not really taken into account the rest of the Act. As you may have gathered, general opinion about something is extremely important in India, and everyone, even in the most hierarchical of organisations, will have conflicting opinions on the most minute detail.

There was a classic moment in my corporate life in India where, with the seconds ticking away before we had to file our accounts, a debate broke out between the various parties, including the accountants and the inevitable lawyer, about the exact sequence that had to be adopted to sign off the accounts. It seemed to be a matter of the greatest importance whether the accountants signed first or last, and the specific order in between. Shortly before I gave up the will to live, I separated the parties, and went to each individually and said everyone else had signed. In this way I got the party in front of me to sign, although not without several stern wiggings to the effect that it should not have happened this way.

The first time this type of debacle happened to me over company administration I was really surprised, both by not being able to overrule anyone, even though I was managing director and I was assuming the full rights of hierarchy, and because the argument itself seemed to have as much relevance to corporate existence as how many angels can dance on the head of a pin. It is salutary to reflect that such arguments can — and almost certainly will — break out on such matters, and it is as well to be prepared for them, though no amount of preparation will actually give you any forewarning what the kerfuffle will be about.

At the barest outline, the process for incorporating a joint stock company in India has a number of stages of which the first is registration. For this you will need a maze of forms all filled in with the utmost care:

- The Memorandum of Association
- The Articles of Association
- Any employment agreements with, for example, the proposed managing director
- A statutory declaration form by a recognised figure that the requirements of the Companies Act have been complied with

In addition you have to have:

- Written consent of the directors, using Form 29 to agree to act as directors

- The complete address of the registered office of the company in Form 18
- Details of the directors, managing director and manager of the company in Form 32

The charter documents of the new company, the Memorandum of Association and the Articles of Association, are significant documents. Take care over their wording.

The Memorandum of Association is compulsory and it is much, much more important than in the West. It specifies the basic constitution of the company and is considered the unalterable charter, and it defines the powers and limitations of the company. Enter details into this carefully. It is a public document and you may find that when you are successful your competitors can cause trouble by their close reading of it.

If there is one step in this whole process that you should take extra care over — it is this one. I have known lawyers in India suggest that I was being too particular about it because getting it right can cause a major log jam, but I knew enough to stick to my guns and get all the indemnities in place from them before continuing.

The Articles of Association are the internal rules of the company, and while not being the minefield that the Memorandum is, certainly deserve some care. Pre-emptive rights over share transfers will, for example, be recorded here.

The textbooks on opening companies in India now usually have some wonderful phrases that contain the most heartache you can imagine. *Be careful to get the exact spelling correct* is one such gem.

You send this little lot of carefully prepared documents to the Registrar of Companies. The usual acronym, ROC, does much to indicate how you will feel, especially if you have any hard places around when dealing with the ROC. You need the fees usually in just the form of currency you do not have, such as a banker's draft. I say fees because the registration fee and the filing fee are separated out in a very Indian bureaucratic fashion. You will need the stamped paper and all sorts of other arcane materials.

The ROC then scrutinises the documents and anything else that is in sight and then following the usual magic phrase: *if nothing objectionable is found,* he or she will issue under his or her seal and signature the *Certificate of Incorporation.* In my experience, however, ROCs are fastidious people and they can find something *objectionable* in a vast array of details within the documents: an ink blot, a slightly misplaced alignment of lines and seals, a slight variation in signature, a failure to number pages, a failure not to number pages, and many other such misdemeanours excite the attention of these people.

If you have any experience of the novels of Charles Dickens and you have a taste for what seems like official sarcasm, you will be in for a treat. If, however, you just want to get on with business, and imagine that India wants you to do so too, you are in the middle of a trial.

The best approach is to leave it in the hands of the professionals. I use a local accountancy practice — by which I mean an Indian practice — and just phone every month or so to check on progress. We once had several of these Jarndyces going on at the same time, and I took to calling myself "Rick" as a way of giving amusement to others.

If you are working in your own country and all this work is being carried on in your name in India, you will have a range of documents to fill in or sign. You then have to have them notarised by a public notary, taken to your country's foreign affairs ministry offices designated for this practice, and you then have all the documents authorised by an apostille. (This is an old word meaning a marginal instruction inserted in the document.) You then have to take the sheaf of documents, and the last time I took it there were twenty four separate sheets of paper which you must photocopy at least three times, to your local Indian embassy or high commission office to have them formally authorised before couriering them to India.

Foreign ministries of all kinds have cottoned on to the fact that they can charge what they like for this, and in the UK it is about £18 per sheet for every sheet having recently been increased from £12, and the Indian embassy or high commission also charges by the sheet, but an obviously much more reasonable £15 or so a time.

I think this reflects the fact that India is a lower wage area.

You have a six months window to get all the documents in once the registration process starts. When you set out you wonder what on earth could take that long. After the sheets have been rejected — in one case because the notary public had not quite aligned his seal with the relevant entry — and the papers start their laborious process of winging their way backwards and forwards to India, you will wonder how anyone can imagine it can be done that quickly.

My obvious question was not concerned with the objections and rejection of my documents as all official bodies in every country exercise that function well, but around the fact that three separate bodies in every country had verified the validity of the documents and all had records of this fact, so why on earth did they have to be physically transported, especially in this day when the Internet has made international business so much easier and so much of the expansion of the Indian business processing offshore business relies on scanning and email.

In response I was regarded with that look that the Indian Administrative Service reserves for those who just do not understand.

Once you have received your Certificate of Incorporation you might think you can get on with business. Not so fast. As a private company you will need a Trading Certificate and if you have a public company you will require a Certificate of Commencement of Business. Leave that to the professionals too — and in due course, though several lifetimes may pass away, you will be up and running.

You can, perhaps, see why forming a partnership as a first step can be quite a good initial move — though you may pay for it in the long term.

The way round the pitfalls are, essentially, low level bribery or having a cousin or brother in law, but as my director in India said, now that some of the process has been privatised even those recourses have been closed off.

Just leave it to the professionals.

Negotiation in India is an art form as much as it is in the rest of the world, with its own peculiar local qualities. The essential element in India is that it is a process of attrition. Having negotiated in the UK, US, France, Germany and Italy, amongst other countries, Indian approaches to negotiation are the most time consuming though, probably the most understandable.

The essential quality is maintenance of one's position, which should be restated in full as often as required. I have solemnly started negotiations in

India with the statement: "For the following 29 reasons, these are the conditions that I must insist on if we are to go forward." I then, equally solemnly, gone through all 29. The other side, favouring brevity, only had sixteen objections to my position, and went through them, in some detail, until I was allowed to restate my original position, in full. My opposite number then did the same with his 16 objections and we went on for eight hours with three breaks: one for food and drink, one to accommodate my independent expert, who did not compromise his independence in any way and steadfastly supported my position, and one to accommodate the opposite side's independent expert who was equally unswerving in his independence and only supported the opposing side.

The great thing about the independent expert is that it does break the monotony.

Failure to mention one of your planks in your argument or your list of objections at the outset of negotiations seems to remove that from the negotiation forever, so be careful to keep going painstakingly through every one of your points.

The great thing about these bouts of negotiation is that winning or losing does become relatively unimportant as thoughts of survival and having a life outside the negotiation room begin to assume some consequence in our mind. It is rather a surprise when you realise that the process has stopped and it is often a surprise to discover what you have agreed, but it does work and the result will stand.

Stand in the sense of being the guiding principle behind the next stage: creating the contract.

In inverse proportion to the likelihood of going to law, the attention to the detail in your contract will be immense. I have metaphorically locked the door on the lawyers and left them to discuss the contracts for days. Ensure any contracts have exit clauses and arbitration clauses, preferably with an organisation you trust, and read any contract seriously and carefully yourself before agreeing to sign. I did have the situation once where, having completed both the negotiation and the process of lawyers being locked together till they agreed, I was presented with a contract that rather varied from what my lawyer had agreed and which I had accepted.

To this day I cannot tell you that skulduggery was at work, but I have my suspicions. If I make light of it now, it was rather shocking at the time and could have been serious.

I have hinted at the role of the government and governments in your business. I did at one stage think that it would be possible to codify the assistance you will receive. (Unkind souls refer to this as interference.) After two years of continuous surprise, with the second year bearing no particular relationship with the first year's help, I have decided that it is best just to wait and see, and react in whatever fashion seems most appropriate.

Chartered Accountants in India are first class as a profession — you will, of course, encounter the usual variations between individuals. The great quality I have found is that they will adapt to your requirements much more easily than in the UK. If you need management accounts in a particular form — because it is what you are used to or this is how head office might want them — this would not be an issue. Accountants in India have to spend so long going round hurdles and finding the smallest cranny within which they can operate, that they are some of the most amazing lateral thinkers in the world.

As with all professions, however, it is useful to know when things are not as they seem.

Alongside discovering the existence of zero, I think Indians have a corner on inverse proportion. The key quality in Indian management accounts that you should look for is an inverse proportion between how apparently accurate the management accounts are and the probity of the accountant. Accountancy at the best of times is an inexact science, with all sorts of judgements about, for example, how accruals are made and when to call revenue cash. It is no different in India, but if there are no discrepancies between the management accounts and the bank accounts, just beware.

I know this happens in the Gulf, because I have experienced it painfully at first hand. I was alerted to the answer of why the company was not doing very well by the fact that the management accounts were absolutely perfect. I could not detect a single error, whether it was between purchase order, voucher, cheque, receipt, totals or the main bank account. It was an absolute picture of accuracy and fraud. The relevance of this to this book is that a goodly proportion of the accountants in the Gulf are, of course, Indian and this was an Indian accountant.

On the other hand, I would not have any more worries about Indian accountants and their probity than I would in the West.

This leads to my last high level warning in this area. Budgets and planning are, of course, closely related, and I will be addressing these areas in some detail later. Just be aware that planning, especially financial planning, is not as important as it is in the West. There is very much a suck it and see approach in India. I have suffered from it personally, trying to reconcile American corporate financial planning schedules, on that typically American quarterly tread mill, with an Indian approach which cannot really see much beyond next week with any certainty, and certainly cannot really understand why looking back at performance has any particular validity.

One client we gave some advice to right in the middle of a project — which they had been handling completely on their own till they got concerned and called us in — was really upset over a change in demands for capital in order to proceed. Instead of £150,000 being required at a particular stage, the company was being asked for £200,000 and, quite naturally, there were real concerns. We did our usual due diligence and followed our usual processes and found that it was what it will probably be most times: nothing to cause particular concern. It was merely a failure to anticipate and budget properly by the Indian partner.

In Indian construction, and projects in general for that matter, there is very much a tendency to have a *that'll do for now* statement. Invariably, that *now* will last for quite a long time, usually forever, which is why the area round a brilliant new office block, magnificent and gleaming marble in the hot sun, can be littered with all sorts of detritus.

In the same way, financial planning can have that same rough edge to it. Just beware!

THE DOMESTIC MARKET

I have already discussed why you should choose India rather than any other country as your main focus for overseas expansion, and in this chapter I will be discussing what it is about the dynamics of the market itself that makes it the first area to consider even if you eventually decide that India is not right for your company. Very often, of course this is not an *either or* decision and it may be that you can take on China and, say, the Gulf at the same time, but for the purposes of this book I am treating it in this way.

The first question our clients ask us about the Indian market is sustainability and it is there that the first easy answers can be found. The second question is why India should be considered for investment against all the other opportunities in the world. The answers to the second question could go on and on, taking each other country in turn. The short answer to that is that when all the facts are put together about India, it does not necessarily mean that a company will always decide to enter the Indian market. There may be, as we have seen earlier, persuasive reasons why other countries, such as China, Russia or the former Eastern European countries look more attractive.

What we have always said to our clients is that whether or not to enter the Indian market demands an answer for most businesses in the West. The answer may well be that this is not right, either in timing or in specific opportunities, but companies should make an informed decision one way or the other.

In understanding the dynamics and attractiveness of the Indian economy and domestic market, there is, of course, the global economy to be concerned with. There will be shocks to the world's economies, including India's, and what looks like an overblown economy in China must have a bearing on what the future economic conditions in India will be like.

On the other hand, some of the statistics about India and its economy begin to paint a picture of a sustainable market where growth and profits look likely over the longer term.

75% of the population of India is under the age of 35.50% of the population is under the age of 25. The spread of the population is not orderly, of course, and this is where some words of caution are required.

In the poorer states where education is of a much lower standard and the various birth control programmes that India has adopted — being one of the first countries in the world to advocate vasectomies — have had less impact, is where much of the younger population lives. To a company wanting to enter the Indian market, these poorer states are not going to be of much interest. Nevertheless, unlike China with its one child policy, India has a very low ratio of dependents to working people, and this gives a picture of disposable incomes if these people have jobs.

India will, however, have a surplus of working age people right through at least into the 2030s and this could be the cause of immense political and social instability. On the other hand, Europe is predicted to have a deficit of working age people of over 10 million as soon as 2015. The US will have a deficit of something like that. Both these figures allow for economic migration, although it has to be said that the figures are not reliable as a sizeable proportion of the immigration is, at first at least, illegal. Other countries, such as Russia, also look to be capable of having a deficit of working age people in the same period.

The key question for India is whether this surplus in working age population is an asset or a drain on the economy through unemployment.

There are huge political and social problems associated with importing people into any country, even to do jobs that need to be done where there is no labour force to do them. A Google search of the simple phrase *importing people to do jobs* generally has around 1.8 million to 3 million hits on average. The opposite phrase *exporting jobs* tends to have a higher range from about 1.9 million to 3 million hits. Not all of them are relevant and not all of them show much understanding of the issues but a lot of the references seem to be very angry about doing either.

I do not underestimate the issues involved. There will inevitably be resistance to moving jobs to India but when you look at the figures it is more than likely that the current trend to outsource jobs to India, as well as import quite a few Indians, will continue, meaning that the economy in India will continue to grow.

In short, the demographics of India look very supportive to those companies wanting to enter the domestic market and there are very few markets that appear anywhere near as attractive.

Currently the middle class in India, which broadly equates to the number of people who speak reasonable English, though there is not a one for one tally necessarily, is growing. There are all sorts of measures of what this means, but a fairly good indicator, at least in terms of purchasing power, is how many people have incomes of between US$4,000 and US$10,000. In 2005 the number was about 40 million households, which is around 215 million people. By 2010 it is expected that this figure will have risen to 65 million households, or 350 million people.

In India this refers to households that can afford to rent an apartment, have a bank account, and own a refrigerator, television and a car or motorbike. These people are essentially only now entering the global market in any real sense.

The value of loans is growing at about 30% per annum by value. Salaries are growing on average by more than 14% while inflation is just under 7%, meaning that there is growth in real purchasing power within the economy.

At the same time, investment in the economy is growing very fast. Reliance Industries, one of the major conglomerates in India, is for example investing over 12 billion dollars in the next few years on gas exploration and pipelines. India is already the second largest producer of cement in the world, and there are still further huge investments in increasing cement production.

ACC alone will increase capacity by more than a third in three years, from nearly 20 million tonnes to nearly 28 million tonnes. Investment in retail shopping malls across the country is enormous, with, for example, DLF, a Delhi based real estate company, investing over 600 million dollars in not only the metros, but in second tier cities.

Every sector of the economy is experiencing growth, as I will demonstrate in a later chapter, but the key element in all this is the demand that is being created. There is a virtuous circle in India at the moment of new investment fuelled by significantly large saving rates within the domestic economy, stimulating more demand and more investment.

Fast moving consumer goods, FMCG, are growing at over 20% and the market for them is worth currently about 17 billion dollars, which is not trivial in world terms. Durable goods are growing significantly as a market:

- Microwave ovens, as a market worth only 174 million dollars, grew at nearly 50% over the previous year
- The automatic washing machine market grew at a rate of 40%
- Refrigerator sales grew at over 10% by value, and nearly 7% by volume to a market size of nearly 1 billion dollars
- Air conditioner sales grew by 50% to nearly 500 million dollars

You may not be in any of these markets, but they are an indicator of what is happening in India and where opportunities are opening up.

Even per capita income has doubled in the last four years to just under $800. This figure is tiny in first world terms, but because of the uneven spread of income, discussed above, it disguises many pockets of real wealth and purchasing power.

The demand for infrastructure that we have already illustrated is huge. There are still restrictions to entry into the India market, particularly around retail, where foreign direct investment is restricted to 51% of any company in the market, and then only to single trademark retailers, but this is becoming an exception.

What this points to for me is that the business to business, B2B, market is the prime target for western companies at the moment in India.

There are certainly ways of addressing the business to consumer, B2C, market or markets. The difficulties however are quite hard to overcome at the moment and the feeling among companies that I have dealt with is that it is still just too early. This is partly bound up with the difficulties of partnering in India with appropriate companies to address the B2C market. While there are any number of companies eager to partner with you, due diligence is just so difficult at this level, that it can cause insuperable difficulties.

On the other hand, do keep a weather eye on how things are developing in the B2C market. Of the nearly 25 million serious Internet users in India, nearly 11 million of them bought online in 2007. This was more than a 75% jump in users buying through the Internet, and when you consider the difficulties of fulfillment, actually getting physical goods to people in India, the figure is stupendous, even if most of the sales were for services like travel. In 2007–2008 the market is thought to be about 1.4 billion dollars having grown from about half a billion dollars in 2006–2007. There is something very seriously impressive happening in India through the Internet, much as has happened in the western world, and B2C companies need to understand the trends, understand the licence requirements and enter the market when the appropriate time comes as quickly and as fast as possible.

My advice is to do the initial research now and be ready.

Nevertheless, at the moment, having spent some considerable time and effort investigating setting up joint ventures for western companies in the B2C markets — a subject to which I will return later — my overall feeling is that it is very much more difficult to be confident of success for the time being.

My focus has been on taking B2B companies through the pain barrier and over the hurdles in order to get them started in India. The need for the goods and services that western companies have is so patent. The need can be in terms of expertise and can be in terms of knowledge of particular manufacturing approaches or it can be in actually the finished goods that can be manufactured in India.

There is quite an important point partially buried in the previous paragraph. In some ways I have found western companies rather reluctant to think about the Indian market in terms of expertise.

I think I understand why now. At first I thought it was fear about losing intellectual property, but there are some safeguards in India now, and they are growing stronger. Then I thought it was a concern about sustainability. My third avenue of thought was about some of the inevitable difficulties about getting paid. Finally I thought it was related to the lower rates that can be commanded in India, so it came down to an opportunity cost.

In fact it turned out to be something of all of those, but the real focus was a disbelief that they could sell expertise in India, and by expertise I mean consultancy of all types. This used to be well founded.

The market has changed significantly now.

The spectrum of consultancy that can be sold in India is very wide. When you look at the scale of construction in India, in ports, shopping malls, industrial units and homes, it is relatively easy to fail to grasp the difficulties Indian companies have in producing these developments to time and to budget. As a property developer in Hyderabad that I am in great admiration of and incidentally very close to, said to me, Indians have the money, they have the training, they have the capability, they have the skills and they have the desire. What is needed is rather more.

What Indian companies lack above all is the knowledge of bringing all of these together. In a rather tortuous search for the right company to set up and work with him in India in property development management, we uncovered a whole range of gaps in the skills in India in each of the disciplines involved, but the overwhelming need was the ability to manage complex projects in the way that western companies do.

At the other end of the scale is a company I have worked with that is in protective clothing and personal protection products. For them the growth rates in individual industries, including of course, construction, were very attractive, but there were three factors that tipped the balance for them.

The first was the way that regulation was being implemented in India. Indian governments have really woken up to the fact that industrial production has to be carried on to world standards, not just those that individual factories can get away with. Inspection of manufacturing plants has moved on and matured from the days when it was just a way of securing a bribe for the inspector. Real teeth have started to develop that the provision of 500 rupees cannot blunt.

The second was the growth in various sectors, which is astonishing. This company sources many of its products from China, so it was natural to consider China first, but it was the growth rates, the real visibility of manufacturing in the economy, that supported the initial reason for considering India first.

The third reason was that there is as yet no single company with market dominance in their market just as there is no market dominance in most of the markets in India. This was coupled with the fact I have discussed at length, that once in there was a high barrier to other entrants and yet the cash cost of entering the market was really low, and the likely return on investment very high.

The demand for goods and services is there and at last logistics and the ability to get goods across the country at least in the B2B world are starting to be mature enough to rely on. The big US logistic multinationals are now in India. They are increasing their services very fast, from a small base admittedly. Travel is exploding in India, as the airlines, new, established and old, fight for an increasing share of a rapidly growing market. We have seen the investment in the golden quadrilateral and what that is going to do to road transport of goods and passengers.

This is a really exciting environment to be in, and the opportunities are vast.

In view of this, my first area of focus for many companies may seem surprising.

Over the years I have seen the way that multi-national companies established in India by parent companies in the West have operated. In the first few years of existence, there is quite a hunkering down and watching process as the market and the Indian situation is observed and analysed. There is a real, often unexpressed, feeling that they are in an alien world and it is quite a challenge. I have no doubt you will feel some of this yourself if you do enter the market, and the largest corporations demonstrate this awareness, even when, funnily enough, they employ locals from the start.

I have seen this as an opportunity for western companies entering the market. If you are already a supplier to a company, probably western, that is established in India, think about what you can offer it in India. In what they see as an alien world, the appearance of an old friend, or at least a trusted supplier, can be a relief and an opportunity. You can also, as some companies I have dealt with have done successfully, be supplied from these companies if they are suppliers to you elsewhere in the world.

The only important warning is that whatever you do, however, do not use any price list you may have agreed in the West — start from scratch and local pricing!

There are all sorts of issues with this approach. I have met many of them and they are not necessarily easily overcome. You will immediately for example be aware that you could be under pressure to use Indian pricing elsewhere in the world.

It is important, however, that you approach the Indian operation in India. I have known companies in the West that have thought that a framework agreement developed with the head office in the West will be very useful. It may be, but one difficulty that can be experienced by any company that wins a global framework supply agreement with a multi-national company is that the framework would not be given anything other than lip service everywhere else in the world. If that is the case, you might as well cut your losses and get on as though it does not exist and just treat the company as any other potential customer. At the same time, of course, do discuss it with head office and see whether any pressure can be brought to bear without affecting your chances catastrophically.

The second difficulty is that even where the framework is recognised there is still within the Indian business soul a feeling that they will not be imposed upon by head office. Having seen this at first hand as the expatriate head of an American multi-national, where my loyalties went both ways at the same time, I realised that it is deeper than I had experienced in any country in Europe where the same sentiments were expressed, even in France.

No matter that Indian business is extraordinarily successful throughout the world and that Indian business people are rightly proud of India's global success, there is still that undercurrent of an inferiority complex in India — a statement that we are as good as them and we do not need this so-called help can be elicited from the most surprising quarters at times. This is not a criticism, just an observation, and even though it is diminishing it is still a potent ingredient in Indian business life.

One reason why it has hung on longer than we might expect is perhaps down to the controlled environment of the first forty odd years of Indian independence, where self sufficiency was the prevailing imperative. Indeed India was long regarded by other developing nations as having the right post-colonial model of development because of its focus on self sufficiency. This thread runs deep in the Indian psyche, and paradoxically is probably all the stronger because the premise on which it was based has proved to be ill-founded. It is instructive to remember that it was almost precisely the moment when India abandoned the idea of self-sufficiency that marked the beginning of India's economic renaissance.

Knowing that this may be part of the underlying business ethos of the local management of international companies in India is a real help in work-ing with them and becoming a supplier to them. You can then use the for-eign head office judiciously to help you understand the Indian organisation, and make any mention of any framework agreement or support from their head office only with the greatest circumspection.

In many ways this is not bad advice in any country but in India it is espe-cially important and with suitable sensitivity this can be a good basis for starting to do business in India.

The key to longer term sustainability, however, is supplying local Indian businesses. With the way that Indian businesses are developing into an international force, working with growing Indian companies is going to be a significant element in your growth. I deal with the processes you might employ in greater depth in a later chapter, but the key issue is your network. If you are first moving to India more or less blind, you will soon rather surprisingly have local contacts which will be more powerful than you might think. All the usual underpinnings of new com-panies will be part of your market penetration process, from bankers to accountants, from lawyers to any of your suppliers. All of these people will offer you a range of contacts and some sort of entry into local business networks.

Choose your bank carefully, for example, especially in terms of helping you penetrate the local market. You will have what is apparently a wide range of banks to select from, but they are all very different, and they may all be part of the same government infrastructure. This paradox is very typically Indian and quite a trap for the unwary. For clients I have used international banks, I have used the state-owned banks, and I have used private sector, local banks. (As some of them have gone international in a much more effective way recently, this may be a misnomer, but the distinction I am establishing is the one we need to focus on.)

The international banks will know you better, or at least understand your perspectives better overall, although it does, as always, depend on the local management. Some of them have been in India a very long time and have good links into local businesses and the local business networks. These are strong advantages and it would be worth assessing the capability of the local branches to see whether they fit your needs. If you already bank with one that is present in India there are compelling reasons to bank with that institution, but I would advise taking stock of other options and assessing them before you make your decision. Although there will be a comfort factor in a strange land of using a bank which has a name you recognise, that is not necessarily what you want.

The state owned Indian banks are enormous and spread everywhere. This, in itself, can be an advantage for you as you grow your business in India. They are, however, a branch of the IAS and as such have the power to move as slowly as anyone can imagine. The beautifully instructive shrug and rolling of the head that characterises the Service can drive you right round the bend as you try to query a payment and its progress through what is known in India as well as the rest of the world as clearing, but in India can really be as impenetrable as an equatorial forest. On the other hand, the quality of the senior management can be staggering, and one of the best international bankers that I have ever met — deeply impressive as a man as well as a banker — works for the largest state bank. The breadth of coverage of India and the fact that they are essentially the way India holds together economically means that you need to assess them.

The privately owned banks, some now big and international, are really very interesting. They are aggressive, entrepreneurial, competent and capable, and creating big changes in India. At a local level they have penetrated small and medium sized business banking very effectively, and their focus can be extremely useful. There are huge variations between branches in a way that may surprise you in this day where in the West bank branches have really become retail sales outlets and have a standardised product, service and feel. There is no substitute for going along and seeing how you are treated and what the bank can promise. In this respect of course, you have to remember that they will over promise and underperform, much like anywhere else in the world, but with this in mind, you will be able to assess what is on offer.

I would not leave the decision about this aspect of setting up in India to anyone else. By all means go along with your accountant or lawyer, and do take their insights seriously, but with my strictures in mind, trust your own judgement. Spotting capability and effectiveness is a good deal easier in my experience than spotting roguery.

I have found that the combination of the local bank staff and the predilections of the companies I am working with are the key determinants in working out which bank is most suitable, so it is not really possible to make a blanket recommendation. The key message, however, is that your bank should be a good way of understanding the local market for your goods and services and should be able to plug you into the local business networks very effectively.

I have sold to both the state owned banks and the privately owned banks and the differences are amazing. It takes a good deal longer to sell to the state owned banks. I really did feel that at the start of one sales campaign I was a relatively young man and by the time we clinched the deal I was old. Once, however, the state owned bank has girded its commodious loins, you are on a relentless trip forward because decisions are there for the long term. With the privately owned banks, the Indian fleetness of business mind means that a decision can be reached relatively quickly — about the same sales cycle as a western bank. That same fleetness of mind can also mean that shortly after embarking on implementation of a project, you are forced into another direction altogether and sometimes even outflanked by a competitor.

It is essential to know what sort of banking relationship and influence in the business community is ideal for you.

The same goes for firms of accountants and, if not so effectively, lawyers. What you are looking for is a set of professionals who want you to do well, who have an extensive network and can get things done and introduce you into the fabric of the business community. In India this is paramount. There are the chambers of commerce, the local branches of the Confederation of Indian Industry and other business networks that you might consider, but at all times be alive to the people who can get things done for you. As I have written before the role of the person who has a strategically placed cousin or brother-in-law is key in so many areas of Indian business life.

Working your way into business in India is not that different from doing this in your own country, except that in your own country you will know the ropes and you will understand what the person opposite means, whether from their body language or inflexion or their general demeanour. There are as many rogues in India as there are in the rest of the world, and the issue for you is that your standard set of intuitive insights are probably not going to stand you in good stead. My rule of thumb is that you should feel uncomfortable when you first start working in the Indian business environment. It should be strange and it should be challenging. If, like me, having learnt over many years how important this is, you love to observe how different things are, you may be at an advantage because most people are looking for the familiar. If you do not feel uncomfortable and you are beginning to think this is not that different from home, it is quite likely that something is awry.

It might be that you are genuinely becoming familiar with the place, but it is far more likely that your opposite number is making you feel at home. As a student of neuro-linguistic programming, NLP, you might feel that this is positive. It may well be positive but I am always wary as soon as I start to feel that India and Indian business is not that different from home. It usually means that someone is playing with my perceptions and if they are doing this successfully, I want to know why. Remember that, unless you are a devotee of Bollywood movies and Indian television satellite channels, your world is a good deal more familiar to your opposite number than the world he or she is representing to you.

It may be that your opposite number is genuinely translating a strange culture and different business environment into language that you can understand, but my experience is that this is a trap for the unwary. If you feel comfortable, you are probably not in the right frame of mind.

I prefer the meetings in India where I am drinking always sweetened, not too distinguished, tea, sometimes without milk, when I have asked for no sugar and some milk. A meeting where we have discussed cricket — a business essential — in a way that requires very little input from me and usually not that much understanding, and we are launched into an improbably rich picture of future affluence completely out of synch with the objectives I have. In that sort of Indian business meeting, I know I am awake, wary and watching, and looking to see how we can match what I have to offer with what the Indian company requires. The meetings that might as well be taking place in Seattle, Paris, Dubai or London are the ones that I distrust.

I am not suggesting, by the way, that watching energetic dancing round the odd tree by quite a few people in a remarkably synchronous way, with cutting between separate scenes of the dance that is bewildering and usually at the expense of the continuity of the picture, is necessarily a good introduction to Indian business life, but Bollywood movies are probably the most accessible form of media to westerners, in the sense that you can find opportunities to see them. On the other hand, if they do not convince you of the differences between India and the West, perhaps nothing can.

That brings us neatly to the role of the business conglomerate in India.

We have cyclical bouts of building businesses in the West that bring together multiple industries where diversity within a business is considered good by the management consultancies. The consultancies, and their allies the investment banks, trumpet the importance of cross-fertilisation between businesses. This is often ramified by the argument that two businesses that have counter business cycles make an ideal match, so that as one goes up, the other goes down, thereby keeping the corporation going. Of course the real moment of truth for that is when both businesses start going down at the same time.

Against the conglomerate business argument is the idea of sticking to one's knitting. This has been the predominant management consultancy orthodoxy for quite some time. It is, however, part of a business cycle or fashion, and I think the private equity, investment bank and management consultancy business view is probably gearing itself up to a more conglomerate feeling in the West in order to stimulate their businesses.

In India, alongside the mass of small and medium sized companies which make up the bulk of the Indian business landscape, there are some behemoths and there is never much questioning of their existence. The Tata Group, Reliance Industries and several others are huge — Tata employs some 400,000 people worldwide, for example, and is in the process of gobbling up a large number of western businesses. I do not want to make too many generalisations about dealing with them as they differ one from another significantly, and different parts of the empire behave differently too. It is seen within the Tata group, for example, that different entities should be what they are, and acquired companies by and large carry on virtually as if nothing had happened.

It would be very true to say that in India great swathes of the Tata Group behave like a branch of the IAS, with whom they are often completely intertwined. Air India was nationalised from the Tata Group as another example. Tata Consultancy Services, TCS, the IT and business processing arm of the Group, has made enormous strides in countries round the world, and itself employs 100,000 odd people. It very often feels in the West like a standard multi-national, which has Indian roots. Then suddenly, wherever it is in the world, it behaves like an Indian multi-national. That distinction may sound like a semantic nicety, but it has real point. In India, where it tried for years to avoid taking too much business because the margins were completely different and lower, it is almost an extension of the Home Ministry. It has layers and layers of people and a hierarchical structure that may alarmingly dictate from the centre in a way that disrupts what is happening elsewhere in the world.

Reliance Industries has been the soap opera, a *Dynasty* for those old enough to remember that television series, for some time in Indian business life. As the family feuded after the death of the founder, there were many watchers who thought that the whole enterprise would implode. How could it survive such a public and emotional destructive force was a question often asked during 2006.

Survive it has done and is even stronger. My experience of tackling part of Reliance as a supplier was instructive, especially given the context of this book.

We have arrogant and self-assured corporations in the West who regard it as a privilege to be a supplier to them. Reliance, or at least the bit that I was focused on, has taken this to new heights. To be a supplier I had to promise that in perpetuity I would supply to Reliance at 15% below the best price my company offered anywhere in the world, that I had to supply proof, and, at the same time, I was not to tell anyone what that price they were paying was — and I think there was more than a thought in the Reliance mindset that this included the accountants back in the US. I could not work out whether this was just one of those things that in India is met with the reply *Yes*, meaning anything that might suit at that particular time or whether this was something we had to take seriously. My sales people said it was serious. The prize was to be a supplier to a company that was a dominant market force in a particular industry right across India. The scale of the difference it would make to the business I was running if we were successful was enormous.

We qualified out. It was not just that I was unhappy at promising something that would be untrue, though that kept me awake, but it was the thought that the business won on these terms was likely to be quite ephemeral. Someone would come and undercut what we had to offer and even if that part of Reliance offered me the business on my competitor's terms, it would be an endless struggle.

I admire Reliance very much and I would not want to generalise from that one experience, but treat my remarks about Reliance and Tata as indicative of the scale of the businesses you are dealing with. By all means think of the opportunity but do keep in mind the difficulty. Their ability to penetrate every part of Indian business life, from entertainment to heavy industry, from management consultancy to telecommunications is extraordinary. They have a lot to learn — a fact which they are beginning to understand and beginning to make strides in understanding — but they are phenomena that have to be appreciated. My advice, however, is to leave quite well alone for as long as you can and only consider being a supplier to them when you can afford it.

If you are taking on one of their businesses as a competitor, they will be awesome and unforgiving and direct. Take them seriously. Although they may look like dinosaurs and slow moving, they can suddenly wake up and move with astonishing speed.

These business houses in India are extraordinary and starting to penetrate the western world very effectively, mopping up steel plants, car production and design, and call centres. Watch them carefully, and be aware of the potential of working with them in India, but also be aware of the fact that the opportunity may become an insoluble issue.

The burden of this chapter is really that the Indian domestic market is extraordinary and is expanding faster than you can almost imagine and at the same time I have been foreshadowing the hurdles to entry, the traps for the unwary and the general difference that you have to keep in mind with India.

My mantra is that if you are working for a company of a certain size in the West, you have to make a decision about whether or not to enter the Indian market now. The cash cost of entry is low. The stress cost is high. The rewards are thin margins now, but the opportunity for market dominance locally, regionally and, perhaps, even nationally. If you decide India is not for you now on the basis of a clear understanding of the size of the market and its growth rates taken against the difficulties, that is at least as important as deciding to take the step.

The one aspect that cannot figure too much in serious business planning of the type that this chapter is seeking to influence is the sheer exhilaration of dealing with Indian business. Keep in mind the difficulties, keep in mind the business days that start at around nine in the morning — well, ten thirty — and finish somewhere around midnight, if they finish at all, keep in mind the sheer difficulty of communication, but also just enjoy it.

FIVE

WHICH PRODUCTS, SERVICES AND SECTORS — AND WHY

S o far we have looked at the general areas of Indian business and the market places in the aggregate. There are huge variations in each of the sectors, and in this chapter we will look at a cross section of them and see how they are developing and the level of maturity in each market. It is necessarily a snapshot to give an idea, and I should reinforce the warning that I do not particularly trust statistics and figures that I get out of India. The figures are useful for indicating trends.

More than anything I also have to restate here how important it is not to see India as a monolith. The various states, the regions, the metros and the various aspects of the paraphernalia of a modern sub continent mean that there is necessarily a level of abstraction in what I am talking about. As you will see in a later chapter there are good ways of working out where you should start your business in India.

I will look at a fairly comprehensive list of sectors that might be of real interest to western companies but inevitably I will omit some areas. My theme underpinning this book is the broad development of India and how to be part of it, and if you think of all the sectors that I am covering it is relatively easy to extrapolate from the examples I give. Where an economy is going through a revolution of a type that the world has not really seen before, in time scales that are certainly new and out of the experience of all economic historians, it needs only a little thought to see that virtually all aspects of a modern western economy are beginning to develop in India, and there are opportunities across all sectors, though the level of maturity will differ and the degree of demand will vary.

I am also arguing against just trying to grasp the low hanging fruit, as the easier wins in any market are generally ephemeral. As soon as they are perceived, they are communicated and the market becomes very crowded for a short period before it settles down. This is, as we have seen, especially true of India. I do not have any major objections to this type of opportunism, and a great deal of Indian business is built on it, but this book has a different function, not only getting into India but creating a sustainable and growing business there.

The businesses that I have worked with that are looking at India as a potential new market come from a wide range. For example there are the professional services businesses, retail businesses, technology businesses, pharmaceuticals in the widest possible sense, logistics, construction, all forms of infrastructure, telecommunications, financial services and engineering. I have looked at high value, branded goods, and what are fast becoming commodity items, such as flat screen televisions, and there is a clear message that has partly changed my perception of India.

It is related to pricing. I had been accustomed to thinking of India as inherently only a low price market. While this is undoubtedly true, it is not universally true.

The main example, just because it is so vivid and challenging, is a comparison of low end goods in the retail sphere and high value, international premium brands and their pricing. Premium goods such as branded clothes and accessories command prices that are, if anything, a few percentage points more expensive in their base, pre-tax pricing than in Paris, London or Washington. Commodity goods are usually anything from about half the price of the equivalent in the West. I thought at first it was just the snobbery value that drove this higher pricing for premium brands, but it is something more than that. There is in India in the B2C market a genuine sense of the value of quality in goods, and this is spilling over into the B2B market in a serious way.

If you look at textile exports from India you will see nothing much surprising as they are at the low end of the market. If you look at the textile imports into India you may be initially surprised that there are any, but you will not eventually be surprised to know that they are significant and they are at the high end of the value chain and that some of the prices charged are indeed higher before taxes than in western capitals.

This is driven by two principal factors as far as I can see.

The first is undoubtedly strong and growing more important by the day and this is the fact that Indian manufacturers and services companies are now competing more than ever in the global market. Even if they are not there yet, there is a realisation that this is the future and that they have to expand out of their own market to be sustainably successful — not to say the fact that usually they can earn higher margins offshore. It is very much the reverse of the stimulus for this book. To compete in the international market, things have to change. Low prices can provoke interest, but gaining a sustainable market share has to be based on something more, and usually that is the quality of the goods.

In 2003, I spent several fruitless months trying to find a manufacturer in India which could produce a certain type of mechanical saw to a high specification. In the end I admitted defeat. The companies that might have had a chance qualified out quickly knowing that their standards were not high enough. The companies that suggested they could meet the specification had either not understood the requirements or had deluded themselves into a false sense of capability. This is not so much the case now. Finding a company that can meet such requirements is still not immediately straightforward, but they do now exist and they do have a real understanding of what quality standards in the rest of the world mean.

The second reason is naturally intertwined with the first. It is that consumers in India are themselves becoming more sophisticated. Foreign travel is still a rarity for even middle class Indians, but enough are taking holidays abroad for a slow permeation of a different perception of quality to have started to happen. There is also a wider perception that fitness for purpose is not necessarily contained in the lowest priced commodity. There is a growing awareness in the Indian market that there may be additional benefits such as durability, that will influence buying decisions. Higher standards are being expected of white goods and consumer durables, and this consumer level understanding is being translated into many B2B requirements.

I think we have to reconsider much of what we think we know about the Indian domestic market because it is changing so fast, and we have to do this on a regular basis — or at least people like me have to do that. A few years ago, I was deeply sceptical about the idea of taking information technology products and services to India. I was conscious that we were taking products and services from a high wage market into a low wage market, but not only that, we were taking them into the pre-eminent software development environment in the whole world.

I was right at that time. Now there are glimmers of interest in the information technology market in India in several products and services developed by western companies. Admittedly these products and services are in general very high end, facilitating the development of IT related consultancy, but the very fact that there is interest is itself quite a new issue.

The mental trick with India is to think of it as a market that is leapfrogging western experience. Even five years ago it was possible to analyse the Indian telecommunications market and to extrapolate future demand for land line telephone equipment from the figures that were available. At least we thought we could.

The penetration across India of landlines was extremely low, with less than 1% of even urban households having a fixed line telephone. Mobile phones — in those days called hand phones in India — were obviously widely used but developments in the market like Internet access looked as though they would drive greater penetration of land lines. Nowadays it is clear that with WIMAX — a wide area wireless technology, satellite or even some newer technology, the whole process of wiring India physically at a local loop level may never happen. On the other hand, India may soon reach

500 million mobile phone subscribers, and the market is estimated variously as increasing at the rate of 5 million per month. The other serious figure that I have seen of 8 million per month looks far fetched but in quantity terms, and social change terms, it is not much more absurd than 5 million a month. In short, while the future has its seeds in the past, the past in technology terms is not much of a predictor of the future.

If you extrapolate from this example into your own industry, and see how the basics of that industry are changing in the West, you will see what I mean. India is not going to adopt a proven technology or solution that is coming to its end of life in the West just because it might be cheaper or the way we would like to think. Do not imagine, in short, that the progression we have experienced of technological changes, management consultancy changes and production changes will be reproduced in India. India is in the fortunate position of not having legacy equipment that it has to change. It is going to leap frog several generations of technological development, especially with its propensity to adopt the latest idea.

Think for a moment about the UK financial services industry which was an early adopter of magnetic stripe cards technology. With a huge installed base using magnetic stripes successfully, moving to chip and pin technology was a major undertaking, and the UK lagged behind most of Europe in adopting the newer system. As a result, the figures for credit and debit card fraud soared well past the rest of Europe and it was that fact that forced the change.

In short India has no real installed base. India can adopt a new approach faster and more effectively and has to have this perspective as a supplier into that market. This is obviously a changing fact of Indian business life because it is now adopting some technologies that will shortly become legacy environments, but for now the market is open.

The challenge is to create a market in many cases, not to serve it with a better product, although both are more than possible.

As an extreme example of how difficult this is, let me illustrate my point from a conversation in India in 2000. The subject is historically limited; the message just the same.

I was discussing the advantages of email with the head of the largest insurance company in the world. It remains the largest, by the way, on one measure — the number of policies. There was a ready acceptance of the advantages if the company had already an installed base of personal computers and a network. The company had neither. On the other hand, at the press of a button on his desk, the CEO summoned a chap into the room, scribbled a note, handed it to him and despatched him to the nether regions of Mumbai. The CEO also said, having demonstrated this capability, that he could have used the telephone.

That taught me quite a lesson in selling in India — the lessons that I thought I knew, which are always the most dangerous.

You have no installed base of virtually anything — apart from this growing number of mobile phones. You have no resistance to change or to new ideas. What you have is a practical streak that will probably throw you back for a moment or two to your early days in selling and the chapter of your life where you focused on objection handling. You will remember that however well prepared you were, there was always an objection that would floor you. That probably does not happen now to any extent, but you will still encounter an objection that you would not have thought of in the West. For example, there is a major block to automation in India, where the argument is that you should never use machines when labour is much cheaper.

Fortunately or unfortunately this is changing, with both labour becoming more expensive and machines cheaper. It is also changing faster than Indians realise — and there perhaps lies the seed that you should encourage to grow.

If I start with the most difficult area, retailing, it will illustrate a truth about the Indian market that is a subtext throughout this book, but which is worth understanding. The political mix in India is extraordinarily varied and by that I do not just mean the coalition politics that rule at the centre and are present in the states. I mean the forces that are brought to bear. Almost without exception US commentators on the retail environment are amazed that here is a country without Wal-Mart. If you have lived in America you can understand the shock this causes. One of the key reasons is the number of people that are engaged in retail shops in India.

Almost 30 million people, about 7% of the working population, derive their living from relatively small retail stores in India and the threat to these jobs that the foreign monsters embody is a potent political force. On the other hand, it has not escaped the attention of the economists in New Delhi that changes in retail distribution and sales are themselves a force for economic development within a country. There is a fine balancing act going on at the moment and changes in the retail industry are on the cards but they are not certain and will not happen that quickly. Nevertheless, Indians as always are finding ways around the stumbling block.

The first way that the industry is changing is that 51% ownership of a single label retailer is allowed in India now. There are some companies entering the market on the back of this liberalisation. On the other hand, the way the majors are starting to grow in India is by warehousing and distribution and the growth in cash and carry outlets is already clear.

It is a low key entry strategy, and should be considered for the future, because although the process of allowing foreign direct investment may be slow, it will happen, and sports goods, building equipment and electronics have already been let in under the 51% joint venture approach. The forces are too powerful for it to be otherwise despite the numbers of voters who stand to lose. If you are in retail or are a supplier to the retail world, now may not be the best time to make a move into India, but now is the time for planning.

From my own perspective I have looked at some of the suppliers to the retail world to see whether it would make sense to enter the market now. I think the balance at the time of writing is against it as the cost of sale is too high. Supplying cash register systems to individual retailers is a labour intensive, support intensive market, for example, and while small companies located within one city or two might be able to make money out of selling such systems, anything of scale will be difficult. There is not enough of a sell once, supply many times environment to make the sales costs sufficiently low to be attractive. I know, however, that companies are looking seriously at the market — in terms of the volumes it requires — and there is a sense that it will not be too long before the sales costs will be manageable.

It is, therefore, absolutely necessary to be poised to enter the market the moment it starts to take off if you have any designs on this market, as a retailer or a supplier to retailers. The overall retail market was about 250 billion dollars in 2005, was worth about 350 billion dollars in 2007, and it is still growing substantially.

The key areas of food, consumer white goods, and FMCG are being examined while luxury brands and coffee chains have already entered the market on a joint venture basis. Even furniture giants, such as IKEA, have established offices in India to ensure they understand the market.

Nevertheless, you will find that the current retail environment in India is really quite astonishingly run on traditional lines. A major wholesaler in Chennai for example, that supplies drugs and other pharmaceutical goods to around 500 retailers, has a computer for billing, but everything else is accomplished with paper and pen. Stock control is by hand. Orders are taken down by hand. The delivery boys are hardly mechanised. There are rarely mistakes and the system works, but it looks quite shocking to a westerner. It is, however, an opportunity.

If you are a supplier to the pharmaceutical industry, you will probably be aware of the major investments in pharmaceuticals in India. About 22% of the generic drugs produced in the world originated in India in 2006 and that figure climbed to 25% in 2007. India has the third largest drug manufacturing capability in the world. There are already more than 30 large foreign pharmaceutical companies in India with a significant presence and foreign direct investment in the industry is growing at more than 50% per annum.

One key to the significant growth is that it is from a low base as it was only in 2005 that India recognised global patents, but it is now a substantial industry in its own right. The change in the market can be seen in that in the first quarter of 2006 Indian companies filed more than 20% of the applications for new drugs in the US. Indian companies are researching and putting into the market new molecules complementing the general perception that it is only generic drugs that are being produced there. I say *complementing* because the Indian pharmaceutical industry is not drawing much attention to this change, but gradually becoming stronger.

Overall there are growth rates of up to 20% in the industry. These growth rates are fuelled by the low costs associated with drug trials and production in India, and they are also an indicator of the scope for suppliers to drug companies. Whether it is packing machines, blister packs or more sophisticated needs of the industry, the market is growing fast and is in many cases working in partnership with the foreign majors. In the previous chapter I have cautioned about the ability to transfer a relationship with a head office into the Indian market, and that caution still stands, but there is scope here to identify the opportunities and to enter the market aggressively by building on whatever relationships you have elsewhere in the world.

At the same time, it is worth remembering that Indian companies are expanding into the global market. They are doing this like Ranbaxy by acquiring rights to sell other companies' formulations in specific markets, or like Sun Pharmaceuticals or Wockhardt buying a complete foreign company, or like Jupiter Bioscience investing in a greenfield site in the US.

The pharmaceutical industry is quite heavily controlled, however, with a Drug Control Policy and Drug Price Control for the home market. The former dictates virtually which drugs can be manufactured, the latter speaks for itself. Nevertheless, the opportunities are significant, if only supported by the export market.

Healthcare is similarly expanding in India, and not just from medical tourism, which is growing rapidly. The overall market is already worth about 30 billion dollars, of which about 80% is private spending, and of that about 90% is supplied by the unorganised sector. The opportunity for organised business to develop in this market is huge.

Medical tourism is built on a number of specialities, such as cardiac operations and eye care, where India has a global reputation for excellence, and my own experience in the Gulf is of Gulf nationals routinely going to Chennai for their health needs. This was initially a surprise to me and when I asked, it was obvious from the response that this was a naive question. In the Gulf, India is the ophthalmic capital of the world.

Some of the development is generated by large businesses in India which have established their own hospitals and other facilities. Becoming a supplier to these groups is worth considering. Medical insurance is growing rapidly as a business. The supply of medical equipment is growing at well over 12%, and is generally in the hands of the international players, such as Siemens,

GE, Philips, Toshiba, Hewlett Packard and Hitachi, and their competitors are creating joint ventures with local companies to enter the market.

Biotechnology is also growing fast and there are about 320 companies in this field, with the top three companies having more than 25% of the market. It is allied with the pharmaceutical industry but has interests in agri-biotechnology and in biotechnology informatics, for example. It seems to me that if you can put *bio* in front of a word and hyphenate it, then India is doing it.

The industry is being actively encouraged by the Indian governments to grow fast, and foreign companies are given real incentives to enter the country and develop capabilities there, with more than 100% rebates for some research functions, for example. On its own this makes the opportunity worth investigating, even if you are like me and worry about the control that follows government money.

Entering the pharmaceutical, health care and biotechnology value chain in India has a great many attractions though the speed with which the sector has moved and is moving means that many of the international companies that supply the industry have already moved into the market or have serious plans to invest which are quite far forward. Nonetheless, this is clearly a rapidly growing market and one that we have seen a great deal of interest in joining.

Moving from one science-focused area to the general area of science and technology, a similar picture emerges of an industry growing initially through low cost research and testing facilities into a fully fledged global industry. In this case, however, there is the added stimulus of the IT industry's success in the global market, which has provided a further stimulus.

Just one measure might indicate the scale of what is happening in India. The number of patents filed by Indians in 2004–2005 was almost 3,600. In 2006–2007 the number will be nearly 5,500. Expenditure on research and development in India was nearly 1.5 billion dollars in 2006–2007, having grown from less than 1 billion dollars in 2004–2005. The areas that are important include space, the nuclear energy programme — highly important to India in view of the current shortage of hydrocarbons — renewable energy, and even oceanography.

As well as domestic research, India is starting to take a more prominent role in international research programmes in pure and applied science.

This is a rapidly growing area which is of direct interest to the Indian government and consequently some of the obscurer barriers to market entry are more limited and entry into the market can be more readily achieved.

The telecommunications market is an obvious one to consider, and one that is quite mature, with even the market for ring tones above 100 million dollars already. As already described, the ratio between fixed line to mobile new users is enormous, with about 40,000 new fixed line subscribers being added a month against the five million mobile users. It is nonetheless a market which suppliers to it ought to have some thoughts about and if they are not already part of it, understand whether they should be or not.

A further closely related area is that of information technology, and some of the adjuncts to that industry are becoming globally important. Semiconductors, for example, are becoming very important to the Indian economy, and it is not only in their manufacture but also their design, as well as the building and delivery of the embedded software that sits in them. India is emerging as a complementary country to Taiwan and China for the manufacture of semi-conductors, and this is based on several advantages, not least the skills available, embedded code development for example, and the government initiatives for encouraging the development of the industry.

If you are focused on selling products or services to this market, then India becomes an important centre in the world market, especially as the market for semi-conductors is underpinned by what is happening in the rest of the Indian market. In 2003, the Indian market for semi-conductors was only 1.8% of the global market. It was 2.9% in 2007 and by 2010 it is expected to be 5.5% of the global market.

The government incentives for companies to enter this market are huge, partly because it is recognised as a building block of India's rise in the global market. There are the Special Economic Zones (SEZs) where manufacturers have incentives such as a 20% contribution from the government to their investment, for example. And this is to ignore the design and innovation units that are being established in India to take advantage of the software engineering and information technology expertise in the country.

The IT industry in India is well known, at least as an export business focused on the rest of the world. The market inside India has been more limited but is starting to grow, and though from a small base, it is growing at high rates, as the need for systems within Indian businesses starts to grow. The personal computer market in India is growing rapidly — at about 20% per annum. It is not a market that most companies would be able to enter, dominated by HP, the local company HCL, Dell and Lenovo but is an indicator of the changing nature of India.

A more important sector to consider is what the Indians call ITES. Exports of IT-related products and services have for years have been tax free for Indian companies, but when business process outsourcing came in, the government took the view that normal tax rates should apply, which meant that anything up to 40% of the profits would go in tax. Getting the law changed in India, even if it were possible, would have taken years. Instead, displaying the ingenuity that only a nation of entrepreneurs brought up in a stifling licence regime would have to learn, Indian companies found the answer. All business processing offshore relies on information technology to be viable. Hence it was an IT *enabled service*, and since it was based on IT, profits from it must be tax free.

This sector is growing very fast and is projected to continue to grow as fast in the future, as the benefits of at least an equally good service at some 40% of the equivalent cost in the West are more and more realised.

This is, essentially, the call centre phenomenon, although I have always resisted focusing on voice as that is the least easy service to transfer to India. It is not so much the Indian accents that are the issue, although some focus is given to them, but it is the lack of domain skills — the local knowledge of how an industry is conducted — which is the key issue for me. The training overhead is huge in call centres even if located in your own country, but compounding that with transferring voice offshore has always seemed to me to be too challenging in the first instance.

By concentrating on reasons why this market should not be regarded solely as a call centre market, I trust that I am directing the focus in the right direction: the outsourcing of back office processes to India. This market is expanding in all sorts of directions, from property management, to insurance services, from legal services to accountancy, from human resources back office support through to simple data entry.

The ability to provide services to the successful companies in this field is important and one that you should consider. The people who work in these back office processing centres are one of the main engines of the Indian consumer economy, being young, unencumbered, with purchasing power that we can only dream of in the West, well aware of the western market and its trends. Selling services to the companies that employ them can be a double benefit, as the agents realise which suppliers they are dependent upon in their local market.

With Indian family structures, and the likelihood that these agents will be living at home — or at least in someone else's home — there is quite an incentive to become a supplier to this market.

A market that I have been involved with reasonably extensively but which is below most people's radar is the training and education market. It is not just that Indian higher education institutions have a world renown for research and teaching excellence, it is the scale of the opportunity for training and education that should be understood.

At the tertiary level, a whole range of foreign institutions are looking at entering India with their own brand new campuses. There are huge opportunities in India for such organisations, as the skills profile in India has not kept pace with economic development. There might be two million graduates every year in India, but they are not all of world class, nor are they addressing the disciplines that are becoming in short supply, whether in India or in the rest of the world. In a parallel move, the Indian Institutes of Management — the IIMs, and the Indian Institutes of Technology — the IITs, are establishing satellite institutions in the Gulf, Singapore, Laos, Cambodia and Vietnam for example. These are initially to serve Indian businesses which are fast expanding their requirements in these areas.

Schooling in India, as we have seen in an earlier chapter, ranges from world class for the elite to less than being visible in some of the rural areas, and yet the government's focus on education from five years up means that the demand for products in this area is set to grow, whether it is whiteboards or services to educators, both of which are growing markets in India.

The need for training is also vast and there are signs that an industry is at last developing, mainly to supply the IT and ITES markets but also the other industries such as engineering and construction. The need for world class standards means that training will become an important industry whereas at the moment it is largely regarded as a part of an employee's job to instruct the person sitting next to him or her. Several business acquaintances of Indian origin have returned to India to set up companies specialising in certain aspects of serving the offshoring market, such as sales and marketing. Like all training markets it is very price sensitive and with its fragmented state in India is one that has a high cost of sale, but it is growing and should be under analysis if you have interests in the area.

Physical infrastructure and construction is evidently a major market if the world's second largest cement market is anything to go by. We have discussed the building of roads, the importance of the development and redevelopment of ports, touched on the importance of the rebuilding of airports and the development of new airports, looked at the construction of shopping malls, industrial parks and homes, and looked at the provision of electricity — where there will be major shortages for years to come — and discussed in outline the needs of the oil and gas industry. If Russia is the major gas station to the western world as an alternative to the Gulf, then India, along with China, is one of the most hungry recipients. If you serve any aspects of the infrastructure and construction industries with any products or services, you have to consider entering the Indian domestic market. As I have said, expertise is in short supply in India, and that is one aspect of this market that companies with expertise should be taking seriously.

I suppose just one figure to add to the list is that the Indian government plans to expand its refining capacity by 62% over the next five years. This is a seriously expanding market, and one that has few dominant players, unlike the rest of the world. The same is true of construction where there are giant firms, but none has a major stranglehold on the industry. It is a real opportunity with a need that the companies within it are aware of.

Automobiles and automobile components are two businesses that are growing rapidly and both are sourcing more and more of the materials locally. Passenger car assembly lines are generally well known to be in India, but commercial vehicles are being made in increasing numbers, with Mercedes, for example, planning to produce buses in India from 2008.

The interest for western suppliers can be in all areas. One of the key areas of growth in the whole market is design, with more foreign manufacturers locating their design facilities in India, close to the car plants. If the design facilities are there, it becomes inevitable that the component suppliers located close to the design studios will have a greater advantage, and so the global reasons for being in the Indian component market start to add up to an imperative. India is not just a country for producing cars and trucks cheaply, but one of the countries where they will be designed and specified, not least because it is growing into a considerable market in its own account while also developing into a leading car exporting nation.

The figures in this industry change faster than a book can keep pace with but with automobile production rising at around 14% compound annual growth rates, it is clear that here is an industry that has to be recognised in the global market.

Manufacturing has long been seen as a minor affair in India, not least because the Indian government talked up its importance years before any reality matched the statements about its significance. There is no doubt that manufacturing, while not in China's league, is growing very fast. The foreign direct investment rates from multi-nationals have increased over the last three years and the demand to set up in India is enormous. Overall manufacturing is probably growing at around 12%, but there are so many imponderables in the figures so that it will be difficult to gauge that. All that needs to be known is that like automobile production, all forms of manufacturing are increasing rapidly. A great deal of the investment is designed to meet consumer demand in electronics and telecommunications, for example, but also in consumer durables. Part of the rationale behind Tata Group taking over the Dutch-UK steel group Corus was that demand for steel in India is set to grow enormously, both for manufacturing and construction, as well as other uses. India is the seventh largest producer of steel in the world — and that is just Indian steel producers in India and takes no account of the steel they produce in the rest of the world.

There is no doubt that China is the manufacturer for the world, but India has a presence and is growing. The industry is relatively new, and starting to build on some of the excellence that is prevalent in other industries. India may have entered late, but it is making a presence in the high end, so it is in design, machine tools, and high quality goods that India is making a mark, and its revenues will grow faster than unit output. Being a supplier in India to that market has to be worth analysis and real consideration.

Tourism and hospitality is a sector that is growing fast, not just on the back of tourists but on the back of the business travellers who are having to go to India to work out whether they should be involved in the country. Suppliers to the hotel, catering and food industries need to understand the opportunities in India. Jewellery is an enormous market in India, and as a mature industry is a world centre of excellence in gem cutting. The market for global information systems — or satellite navigation — is growing in India at a huge rate, as is the demand for real estate services, which can be directly related. Financial services are being liberalised — insurance slowly for domestic protection reasons — but suppliers to these markets need to be aware of the potential.

The industry that is the most challenging is agriculture, partly because of the uncertainties caused by international trade barriers. Water is a key resource, and availability of water is fraught, with states having disputes when one higher up the water cycle takes more than the coastal states think is appropriate. There are all sorts of ramifications to this industry, but training, agri-chemicals, and protective equipment are three where I have had a direct interest over the last two years. Indian companies are starting to take a greater interest in the agricultural sector, and, as I have said, always keep an eye on where Indian business people are placing their bets. If the international trade talks and decisions start to turn in India's favour this could be a major market opportunity.

There are a number of warnings in this area, as the vagaries of Indian farmers cannot be underestimated. I am indebted to one of my colleagues in Chennai for the following insight. In Orissa, a state in the north east, there was a scheme to use the fertile land there to grow sugar and to build sugar mills. In many ways it was a foolproof scheme. The mills would give the seed to the farmers who would harvest the sugar and be paid for their efforts when they delivered the crops. Instead of growing the crops, the farmers quite naturally sold the seeds, making an immediate return, and the whole scheme fell apart.

Finally there is Bollywood — and this is an area that is fascinating, mainly because Bollywood is a major element in a much more diverse industry. I have pointed out the impact of television liberalisation, but there is also radio, and the range of foreign programmes that are used. Animation and advertisements can be more cheaply produced in India, and they have a synergy with the IT and communications industries that makes them an attractive market. If you are in any of these fields or supply into these markets, India has to have attractions.

This breakneck ride through some of the sectors in India has probably confirmed what most people suspected — that the Indian market has many facets and many that are growing fast, drawing in products from the world and creating new demands. What should not be forgotten is that Indian business is, unlike China's, dominated by services. The ratio is not comparable with the West, where typically services account for 80% of the gross domestic product, but services and demand for services are still significant, accounting for some 55% of the market.

Some of the services are ones that we have briefly discussed above, such as hotels and communications, but, there are also the transport and travel sectors — with airlines being ever more important. If you take one message from this chapter apart from the astounding growth and opportunity that lies in India, focus on what services you can provide, because it is that part of the market that many of the more easily satisfiable elements for western business can be found.

In short think first of advice and consultancy as a significant part of your potential offering in India, and think of that as a major building block for establishing a sustainable business there. It also has the advantage that it commands a premium — not perhaps the rates you are used to in the West, but certainly a premium in Indian terms.

Where there is a growing market of this kind, scarcely imaginable a few years ago, there will be companies drawn in for the short term and trying to make a quick buck. I trust, however, that I have made enough of a case for you to think of the longer term potential, when, for example, growth has slowed to, say, six per cent per annum. Even that seems quite tempting — and it is what the sustainable future looks like in India.

SIX

BARRIERS TO ENTRY AND HOW TO OVERCOME THEM

A fter all the preparation in the previous chapters, it is good to take stock and understand how to go forward. I mean by that that we should look at the impenetrable qualities in India and how to overcome them — or at least be aware of them.

The biggest barrier to entry into India is the cultural divide. It is both the ordinary cultural divide — just the normal, very different perspective on life — and the business cultural differences that will call you up short every time you meet them. It is that moment when you wish the ground would open under your feet because you realise that what you take for granted is perceived completely differently from how you intended it. The everyday cultural moments are too numerous to worry about. You will just have to make the mistakes and apologise. The business cultural differences can be mostly planned against and although there will still be the dangers, you can at least work out ways of dealing with them.

The first step to making progress with the business culture in India is not to take *yes* for an answer. In any culture the language equivalent of yes can mean a wide variety of things. In India, as I have illustrated earlier, you just have to take the word as meaning virtually nothing. If you paraphrase it as meaning that I am in the same room as you, I have understood perfectly what you have just asked me and I am making a completely non-committal answer in saying yes, you will just about have grasped what yes means in business circles in India. It is no exaggeration, although it sounds it, to say that yes in such a context is not even as definite as non-committal.

I think my worst experience of the use of yes was one late night in Mumbai, which does not, of course, identify it particularly uniquely. I had said that if I had to leave the country without a signature on the contract, then that was the end of the matter. I could not hold the offer open any longer. We had talked each other out through sixteen hours and I finally had had a real yes from the Deputy Managing Director, who was the signatory. At least I took it as a real yes, and I asked as much, and he confirmed that it meant yes.

We went downstairs to finalise the last few changes in the document that we had agreed. In my client's project manager's office, I met a brick wall that meant that while the Deputy Managing Director had said yes, he had not meant yes in that sense. I must say that a little irritation entered my soul and I asked, first through narrowed lips, then louder, in what particular sense of the word yes had we all meant yes? This was followed by a very long stare from me and a very long stare back from the project manager, which, to date, has been my only experience of silence of any form during negotiations in India. The trouble was that I knew that in all likelihood, the project manager was right.

I think the fact that we did get the signature and that I did get my flight was because the project manager felt sorry for me not understanding such a simple little word like yes.

The other trap for the unwary, although it is more of a trap for some cultures than others, and I find the Indian approach very akin to working with the Dutch, is that the Indian approach to questions is to answer them precisely and exactly as they perceive the question.

For example, my question about whether my Indian opposite number had ever had this problem with this situation was truthfully answered. *No such problem had been encountered.* Were they sure? *Absolutely, positively, never had they had that problem in that situation.* Never? *Never.*

I was astounded. It took me about twenty minutes of asking the same question in different ways and different questions in the same way to realise that they were in fact truthfully answering the question I was asking. So I asked them whether they had ever been in this situation. *Never.* Which is why they had never had the problem.

With these two little devils, of *yes* and answering the question they perceived me as asking, playing around, added to the complication of the different use of language, you can understand why your discussions with lawyers in India will be rather fraught. They will not like to answer anything except with a yes, if they can help it, and they will answer the question that you ask.

The only way round this is that you have to be extremely precise yourself.

When I explain this to clients, there is usually a sense of frustration and impatience. There is partly a feeling that they always are precise, partly there is a sense that everyone else in the world understands what they mean when they speak. That is fully understandable. I suppose my approach to this, based on my fascination for language, for business etiquette and for the idiosyncrasies of life, is not really normal.

Over the years I have looked for a compromise between my extreme view and my clients' usual response, or at least a rationalisation of the two. The best one I have come up with is that when entering on a new business venture the more clarity and precision you have, the better it will be.

In dealing with Indian lawyers and the Indian legal system, just look for ambiguity in anything you say and try to eliminate it. You will have had enough experience in your own country of not communicating precisely what you mean to know the difficulties, at least in theory, but in India the problems will be worse.

Take the rather simple phrase *by Friday*. In any culture, you will not know whether that signifies you want something before Friday starts, by midnight on Friday or somewhere in between.

Remember the Indian sense of stretchable time, and you will see that the phrase takes on another dimension. I was delivered a report I had asked for a week late. I had not specified which Friday — and I could not deny that it was Friday and I did have the report. At the time I do confess that I wondered whether I had been taken for a ride, and I probably was, but that did not stop an entire senior management team finding it extraordinary that I should have put the interpretation I did on that phrase. As one said to me, absolutely straight faced and only rolling his head a little in deference to my inability to understand that bit of body language, "If you had meant last Friday as the day you wanted the report, I am sure you would have said and made sure it was understood."

I eventually grasped the rationale behind this. Before the Friday I meant, it was probably a shared understanding that it was the next Friday. After that Friday had passed, and I had not immediately mentioned the fact, it seems obvious to an Indian that I meant at the very soonest by the next Friday. Despite their long and glorious past, and perhaps because of it, Indians really do not look back, and so trying to reconstruct what was meant some time in the past is just not worth the effort.

I am assured that the following is not apocryphal by the Indians who claimed to have been involved in it, but it is difficult not to find it unbelievable and quite difficult for a non-Indian to construct what the original sentence was, though I think I have nailed it down after years of thinking it through. An order was placed which was meant to ask for five thousand fashion shirts, half with long sleeves and half with short sleeves. The result was five thousand shirts, each with a long sleeve and a short sleeve.

I think the order must have read: "Five thousand shirts, half the sleeves long and half the sleeves short." You can just about see how that would lead to confusion, especially when you enter the mind of the Indian factory owner who would regard western fashions as being odd at best and entirely likely to specify something so bizarre.

The point is that you will inevitably make mistakes and the trick is to get the lawyer opposite you to tell you what he understands you to have said. He will probably repeat your words, but remember that he will be putting his or her construction on your sentence. You need the lawyer to paraphrase what you have said in order to check that you both understand something in the same way. It is not infallible, but it is the one safeguard that you have got that you are communicating reasonably effectively.

This is one reason that contracts and all legal affairs will take so long in India. I have spent more than two days going through what I thought of as a rather simple non disclosure agreement. I bow to no one usually in my ability to be a pedant about language but I do bow to Indian lawyers. We saw enough ambiguity in each phrase to delight any intellectual puzzling over James Joyce's *Finnegan's Wake*. Be prepared for the fight to the death over each clause and phrase. And do not imagine that words mean the same in Indian English as in your English. It is often said that the US and the UK are divided by a common language. This is as true of India and the US and India and the UK.

The real issue for westerners comes with words for time. Simple words like soon and shortly have a life of their own and mean something relative to whatever concept of time the Indian is currently thinking in. It could be normal, Indian standard time, IST, which is commonly Indian stretchable time. In this case the two words can encompass anything from a few minutes to a decade or two. It could quite easily be geological time, however. If you want some sort of insight into how difficult this is to understand all the time, I was still surprised, after years of dealing with Indians and their time keeping, when the first guests for a reception, who arrived not less than sixty five minutes after the time the event was due to start, were greeted by the host with the words: "I just knew who would be early."

Absolutely no irony was intended or taken.

On the other hand, I have found that a signature on any document is binding in a way that many westerners might find restrictive. It works both ways of course, both for your signature and for their signature. I am not suggesting that anyone casually signs anything in business, but certainly do so in India with real care. If you put your signature to a document, it will be regarded very seriously and be a matter of real concern. The clue to that is in the care taken when preparing any such documents. It is not because they will be produced in court — that is hardly an option as I have indicated, though it is getting better — but because they will be used between parties who are getting on well. It is an old western adage that if you need to re-examine the contract, you have not got a viable agreement any more. In India this is not the case. All sorts of documents, including the most casual letter can and will be produced.

I have found Indian lawyers to be first class professional people, with whom you can work closely and effectively, albeit slowly. In western business life, I have found two types of corporate lawyers. There are those who can find every reason why you cannot do something, why what you are asking is outrageous and probably illegal, and who knows every statute and issue that will stand in your way. Politely and firmly, and sometimes just firmly, they ensure that nothing can possibly happen, if you take their advice. I sometimes wonder whose side they are on, and when I wonder this aloud, it turns out that they are on no one's side, but they do have to uphold the legal structures.

On the other side is the corporate lawyer I worked with once who saw it as his job to find a way through the legal minefield to achieve what we wanted at the same time as mitigating all risks. As he was the first lawyer I worked with, I thought they were all like this.

It is my experience that Indian lawyers are very much like this. They are the most mentally agile lawyers I have ever encountered. I think it is because the law is so complex and unwieldy in India that the only way they can survive is by being flexible and looking for loopholes and odd ways through. I admire them immensely.

Nevertheless, it is accountants that will be your best allies in India among the professional services that you must use. You can expect them to be extremely able in adding up columns of numbers and spotting anomalies in your figures, but, much more importantly, you can expect them to know a great deal about the ways round all the obstacles in Indian business life and also to go far beyond their own apparent circle of interest.

Like accountants the world over, they are not necessarily the best communicators. Defeated by a round of baffling bureaucracy, I was rather despondent one evening. The accountant came over and could not understand why I should be feeling so down. I told him the sorry tale. He did not blink an eyelid. Yes, it was true that I had done all that, and I had to do it, but he could have told me what the result was. It was by no means negative. I had now ensured that the next level of engagement would be set in train and we were on our way. I had to cheer up as we had made enormous progress.

I asked him what he meant by saying that he could have told me that the whole day would be wasted but I had to go through it as a sort of rite of passage. He looked at me with no comprehension. It turned out he had not told me because he knew it would be like that. I realised that there was probably no way I could explain to him that that was precisely why he should have told me and have it understood.

That is why I always advise people to find the best accountant they can in India and work with him or her very closely, but always ask the accountant every question you can possibly think of asking, especially about outcomes. On their advice I have trailed across Delhi, gone into some offices that reminded me of Dickensian London, acquired bits of paper with all sorts of rubber stamps on them, and met the most alarming officials, one of whom had two henchmen with machine guns looking very nervously around them the whole time. I have wearied my way across Mumbai — a very different experience from the high speed thrills of Delhi and more akin to torpor than anything else — ensuring that various cousins and shady relatives have all been met and greeted, and in most cases, I have achieved the purpose that I set out with, thanks to the accountants.

The best networks of contacts throughout the IAS are maintained by accountants. They have cousins and brothers-in-law everywhere.

I have explained that negotiations in India are long drawn out affairs. Whatever *Negotiation 101* course you have done, you will need to have it at your fingertips in India. The normal idea is that you must have the clearest possible view of what you want and you should know precisely what your sticking points are and where you can be flexible.

In India this will hold true. The precise understanding of what you want to achieve, formed ideally in the cut and thrust of a meeting with your accountant where you rehearse everything, and ask every possible question, is absolutely vital and vital in a way that will test your understanding of that word *vital*. Negotiation, as I have said, is siege warfare, where you must state, restate and then state again what you want to achieve. Your opposite numbers will do the same and you will do this for hours and hours, at least it will seem like hours and hours, and, in all likelihood, it will be. Do not deviate or hesitate. Just state clearly the terms of what you want. As in any siege, the slightest weakness will be pounced on by the other side, adroitly and almost before you know it. But just keep on relentlessly stating your case, and all supporting facts and figures that you need.

The issue of knowing where you can be flexible is important to grasp because at no point when you are introducing the idea of slightly moving or shifting your ground must you admit that you are doing so. My best salesman was primed to introduce the idea that we would be able to bring forward delivery if certain key elements in our demands could be met. This was a substantial alteration in our stance and it did involve some risk, but we had agreed it might be used if we felt it would gain the advantage we needed. I realised after he had brought it forward, that he had done so in such a way that it sounded as though he was being more obdurate, not less. He said: "It is undeniable that we cannot bring forward delivery, and while you are not asking for this, under certain circumstances we could do so as part of our existing statement of our best and final offer."

As a statement of logic it does not bear much hard analysis, but as a tour de force of Indian negotiations, it was exceptional. The response proved it. The immediate question came back: "What do you mean by saying that we do not want to bring delivery forward?" By making our change in this way, he had in fact made it seem as though they had changed their minds. I do not recommend western minds to think too much like this as you will not be able to reproduce this logic, and if you do, you will be condemned by head office for thinking like an Indian.

On the odd occasions when I did manage this feat, I was.

My Indian readers, I assure you, will puzzle over this bit and not see why it is exceptional.

When you have started to be able to achieve sales and get through negotiations in India, you will need, as in any culture, to understand your customers and clients better. In western business culture I have used corporate hospitality to good effect. It is, by the way, usually known by me as corporate hostility because of the difficulties it can cause internally, especially ensuring that the right people are invited, accept and then turn up. In India I have found it an absolute minefield and my advice is to adopt a different approach until you are very familiar with Indian norms and customs — and even then treat it as a very different animal to anything you have encountered in the West.

If you are entertaining over dinner, for example, there are simple pieces of advice, such as starting to eat your meal as soon as it arrives, and not waiting as the British do for someone else to start. Worry far more than you would in the West about the guest placings round the table, and try to ensure that there is parity in levels between the people sitting next to each other. The real problem is that such meals are incredibly stilted as there is no short hand for putting each other at ease. The benefits are usually pretty thin too, as it is hardly normal practice.

Over time, I have discovered that Indian business has another way, and I recommend it. Business meetings in the West are, unless otherwise signalled, generally an hour. In India they cannot be assumed to last that sort of time. It is after the conclusion of the meeting, which can in any case take an age as you agree the final actions and then agree them again, that the opportunity arises. I have found it is perfectly possible to extend the meeting for anything up to an hour, getting to know my opposite numbers and talking in a non-specific way about anything and everything. Of course the main subject will be cricket, which is a bit tricky if you are American or European, but I have seen conversations taken quite a long way by asking whether the Indian national team will do well in the next tour, though I am perfectly sure that not much information was actually transferred from Indian to westerner.

Out of such discussions you will learn a great deal, both about the individual you are dealing with and about the business environment, though probably more about the latter than the former. I try to ask general questions about India and any issues that I know are of concern. I am fascinated by arranged marriages, by the caste system, and by the general Indian attitude towards the law and the police — and I find that these questions are usually good ways of starting to get to know somebody in India. Once you have had a few of these with the same person, you will find that they will be valuable and become more interesting and you will genuinely learn something about the other person.

There is another purpose to these conversations and one that you should remember over and above the usual reasons for wanting to understand how a client or customer, potential or otherwise, thinks and works. Remember that in India you will need to build your own network as fast as you can. It might seem a little cynical to burden such end of meeting pleasantries with another objective, but it is almost expected. There is a real sense in India that business can be so awkward that you need to cultivate all sorts of people even if you only have the vaguest sense that they might be useful to you one day.

Your opposite number will definitely be thinking like that. He or she will almost certainly have an eye on various aspects of western markets and you might well be the key to unlocking some opportunities in the West.

Indeed you might. In cementing your relationship you may be able to create other value for the Indian business people you meet, and it is something I recommend my clients to keep in mind. If you remember that every Indian business person you meet is likely to have a trader mentality, you can see where the mind set is and where it might go. This can be very much a win-win for both sides and some unexpected alliances have been formed to work reciprocally like this. The usual caveats apply. Not least about focus on establishing yourself in India being diluted by such examples of serendipity, and about doing due diligence on your opposite number, because there are as many unsavoury characters in Indian business as there are in the West, but I have seen some significant ventures created from just such an opportunity developed by both sides.

I have stressed the importance of the network enough, but this last point raises the issue about developing your own network of contacts and moving beyond piggy-backing on the networks created by others. In terms of barriers to entry to Indian business, the lack of a network is a major one. Without it you will struggle far more than you need. The opposite is true, however, and once you have a network of contacts and people who will know the right people, you will have created a massive barrier to entry for your competitors who will have been eyeing what you do. Of course it cannot occupy your whole time, but any time spent embedding yourself in the local business environment and meeting other business people, bureaucrats and professionals will be time well spent. Bureaucrat, by the way, is not, as it can be in the West, a term of abuse, but just a job description.

And if you are like me, you will enjoy it. Over the years I have had virtually no time off in India. My only tourist destination was the Taj Mahal — which is beyond words and worth the ten years that were taken off my life by the hair-raising car journey I undertook to get to Agra — in all the years of engagement with India. The working days will tire you out and they will go on forever.

Getting to know Indian business has no rival excitement in my business life. Getting to know Indian business people has been a challenge, equally exciting, bewildering and astonishing by turns. It is also frustrating, beyond understanding and hilarious.

The secret I have found is to embed yourself in the culture. Think like an Indian. And when you get back to the West, be prepared to be astounded by the decisions you made — but know they are true for India, even if they do not travel so well.

But whatever you do, do not think like an Indian when you get home. That really just does not work!

SEVEN

CREATING THE BUSINESS CASE AND THE BUSINESS PLAN

So far we have endeavoured to explain why India is so attractive as a market to enter and create a presence in, with the opportunity to create a dominant role as there is so little market dominance in India at the moment. We have also indicated some of the difficulties, some of the hurdles and some of the problems establishing a company effectively in India and how to address these issues. Now is the time to be more specific and to provide a framework for dealing with the process of entering India in business planning terms.

Any view of India will show that there are great reasons to get there and establish your company. My starting point with my clients is that this is not enough. It has to be right for a particular client.

We have worked with clients who decided for good reason that this just was not the option for them, but, as I have stressed, making that decision on an informed basis is vital and it is relatively difficult. The difficulties arise because we are very conscious that the real cost that we cannot actually quantify for any company is the opportunity cost. By entering India you are possibly — if not probably — limiting what you can do elsewhere and these other opportunities are the ones that you have to count. These pages there-fore take it as read that India is an extraordinarily attractive opportunity for all western companies of a reasonable size. They do not take it as read that for your particular company it is either the best opportunity or one that you cannot turn down.

We approach this issue with our clients in a very specific way that this chapter will, to some extent, reproduce. We work through a set process. What this chapter cannot do is provide the answers in quite the way that we work with clients in a live setting to do. I guess the most productive way to read this chapter is therefore as though it was a dialogue, with me providing the questions and you providing some of the answers. If the answers are broadly positive, we can smoothly move towards creating the business case in outline and then the framework for the business plan.

We generally create a two or three day workshop for our clients — if it is three days we are able to work in more detail, but both programmes cover the same ground. The level of seniority of the attendees is vital and we have found that unless we have a board level sponsor the workshop is probably not that much use. The impact of what we are potentially planning is such that most of our clients choose to have at least a subset of the board in the sessions.

At various points in this chapter you may say to yourself as, invariably, and I mean invariably, my clients say to me at some point in the workshop, that they do not have enough information or knowledge to create a business case this soon. The reason why you will probably come to this conclusion, and the reason why my clients do, is that you will be right, just as they are right. You will not have enough knowledge or information or experience.

But you have to start somewhere, and I have learnt that the following approach is a very good way to start. As you will see, what it does show, not more than anything but certainly very clearly, is what you need to know.

My starting point is always to create a common understanding. To do that we start by sharing the objectives we have which are to:

- Cover all the elements that must be considered in order to enter the Indian domestic market successfully

108

- Identify the way forward that is most appropriate for the company we are focused on
- Consider the costs involved and the opportunity costs
- Create an outline business plan, and the measurable objectives
- Create the essential elements of the business case so that your company can decide whether to go forward and enter the Indian domestic market

As part of this we generally advise that we should do some market research addressing the markets that the company itself might be interested in prior to the workshop. In general this is not a major exercise, amounting to two or three days work looking at trends for particular industries and giving some idea of the best locations in India.

You will have seen the focus on expertise as a key product or service area that western companies might be able to sell successfully in India and we look at the possibilities for this as well while we are doing this desk research. Of course we mostly do this from our company in Chennai, but that is not essential, just cheaper.

The opening session is more or less the ground that we have covered in the first six chapters. The idea is to create an understanding of where India is and where it is going in the next five years. The second session is devoted to the details of the Indian domestic market, looking at what the market drivers are and how this market differs from mature markets like Europe or the US. We bring in the fact that there is usually no installed base of very much that is important, and that therefore we are starting with what is effectively a clean slate. We find this surprisingly difficult to convey adequately, partly because, we have come to understand, this is such a strange concept. It is a simple enough idea but it is so far from the experience of senior business people in western companies that it takes some getting used to.

At this early stage it is useful to start the process of understanding which market drivers are useful to you. I conduct an open session, inviting people to pick up on what I have said, anything in the pre-reading that I have sent them and other information that they might have found for themselves, and we assemble a list of the market drivers that might be important to them as a company. As you will see below, I try not to make my question closed in any way, and invite contributions from any perspective. (In the usual definition a closed question is one that I know the answer to before I ask it.).

Depending upon the industry concerned, the range of market drivers can be wide or narrow, but most company's senior management teams look at the growth of spending power, the size of the consumer market and how it is growing, the fact that the market is usually quite fragmented and there will inevitably be consolidation or the opportunity to create a dominant position, customers in the West who have a presence in India already and who could be clients in India as well as the West, and, for example, the return on investment that will be possible, especially as the actual investment may be quite limited. We also look at the presence of any western competitors in India. The idea is not to have a consensus but to stimulate thought, and to encourage people to use almost what they do not know consciously to begin building what they do know.

The list that we create is useful later both as a basis for more discussion and as a check list on whether perceptions are changing through the workshop.

My next step is to see whether at this stage we can look at the market drivers in terms of the company that I am dealing with and see how they fit together. This question is useful in its own right, but then more useful as we consider the next but one set of questions.

As one example of a list of such market drivers the following might be of interest, bearing in mind that it was from a particular sector:

- Health and Safety legislation
- Implementation and compliance with that legislation
- Concerns within India about future requirements for safety and health
- Quality requirements in compliance
- Product standards
- Amount of people already working in the target sectors and the predicted growth in the numbers of people
- How the market is served: is it currently fragmented and to what extent

- Expertise held by the western company
- Thought leadership to be provided by the company
- The fact that the company is a western business
- Foreign Direct Investment (FDI) in the sector
- Western companies entering the Indian domestic market need to have common standards with their own domestic operations and will they also have a predilection to use companies that they already have confidence in
- Exports from India will have to come from companies that use high standards
- Indian business growth
- Multi-National Companies (MNCs) already in the Indian market
- The company has:
  o Reputation and branding
  o Consumer pressure in the Indian market
    ■ Export and domestic
  o Value engineering
- Return on Investment for Indian companies if they use high quality goods
- Western credibility in general

As you can see it was highly specific, but do note the way that the company's qualities became interweaved with the drivers in the market place, and although this does not happen in every case, it is quite useful when it does.

We follow this by looking at the various ways of entering the market, from scratch, through some sort of co-operative agreement for an Indian company to build your capability, operate it for a defined time, and then for it to be transferred to you, a partnership, a joint venture or, finally, through a distributor. (We examine this aspect of entering the market in more detail in the next chapter.)

Then we use a very old device and one that I have tried to stop using as it seems hackneyed when you have used it as often as I have. The truth is that even if you habitually use it, it throws up enough issues and concerns to make it valuable every time. It is the SWOT, the process of looking at the strengths, weaknesses, opportunities and threats that your company may face in entering the market in India.

I use a sleight of hand when I am doing so. You may have immediately realised that there are various perspectives that the SWOT could adopt and therefore this will skew what people will identify. The SWOT can be focused on your company's strengths, weaknesses, opportunities and threats in isolation from any consideration of India, or on those that the company faces in entering the Indian market, or even, indeed, as one or two people have perceived the question, what are the strengths, weaknesses, opportunities and threats in the Indian market itself. I say that I use a sleight of hand here because unless I am challenged, I do not elaborate, and I watch to see how people answer. My perspective is that there are no right answers, only answers that will help us understand whether the Indian opportunity is likely to be successful for a particular company.

What generally happens is that the first two perspectives at least get muddled up as people struggle to write down their answers, and the results are quite revealing. For example a strength that was identified on one occasion was the fact that the company knew its markets in great depth and another strength from the same person was that the company was adaptable especially when it did not understand the market. These are not quite contradictory, but they did tease out some qualities that might not have become visible if I had insisted on a particular focus when the people were writing out their suggestions in each category.

You might find it useful to approach the creation of the SWOT in the way that I do. I first ask for everyone concerned to identify up to four strengths that would be relevant and to write these down. As I say, I try to leave it as open and as free as that. Sometimes I am pushed to be more specific, and I will generally own up to not knowing what I want, only that I need each individual to interpret the question, knowing there are no right answers as I am not looking for anything in particular, not a theme or a focus, just insights into the way the senior management thinks.

There are obviously key words or phrases that might be of value, like adaptability or willingness to experiment, but sometimes those strengths are automatically thrown up by the fact that I am questioning the company's strengths in what is a relatively closed environment.

If I go back to the example I used above of what the strengths were, as we discussed the various strengths identified, it became clear that knowing its market thoroughly was a key element in the company's ethos and behaviour, and this was extremely useful in building the business case and ensuring that it received the right sort of analysis. In short, the strengths can give a great many insights into the self-confidence of the company and whether that self-confidence is well based.

In general, having asked everyone to give their understanding of the strengths and writing them up so everyone can see, there is usually an enormous debate about the strengths and even about shades of opinion within a particular shared view of a strength. An example from the many that we have conducted was whether the fact that the company was hugely cash generative was a strength or not in this situation. Some people could not see the relevance of this quality, some could not see why being cash generative in one market was a transferable strength, others had a view that being cash generative was almost a state of mind and that it was therefore important to create this ethos in a subsidiary, while others saw it as a strength because it meant that the company would be able to absorb losses in India until the Indian subsidiary became successful.

You may be able to see how being so cash generative was immediately seen as a weakness in this context by the finance people, because it seemed to imply that it did not matter what the losses might be in India.

As an example, here are some strengths identified by one company looking at itself. (In order to ensure some sort of consistency through the examples, I have mainly taken the following lists from the same workshop.)

- Intellectual Property within the company
- Web system and presence
- Expertise in all aspects of this business
- Long termism

- Earned reputation
- Thought leadership
- Relationships with customers
- Relationships with suppliers
- Longevity
- Diligence
- Commitment
- Values/ethics/integrity
- Energy and enthusiasm
- Added value to customers from working with the company
- Cash generative
- Sound P&L
- Risk aware
- Brand
- Company communicates well with its staff, suppliers and customers
- IT platform
- Operational decision making
- Market:
  - Size
  - Growth
  - Immaturity
  - Competitiveness
  - Environment

Forcing the discussion away from what can be very general strengths or strengths that are not applicable in a different market, towards identifying the relevant strengths — again with no right answers — is another useful stage in creating the understanding of whether the Indian opportunity is one that the company will whole-heartedly embrace.

What I am alluding to here is a paradox that often occurs at this point. Out of the discussion of the company's strengths, particularly at this point as we relate it to the specific question of entering the Indian market, most management teams start to feel that while India might be a good idea and a major opportunity, and while they have plenty of strengths, the moment is not right.

I have looked at the psychology of this many times and the best that I can come up with is that their perception of strengths is based on self-confidence and self-confidence comes from understanding and what starts to emerge from the process is a realisation of how many unknowns there are.

This may not be the only reason or even the main one, but it does help.

I say it is a paradoxical reaction because when shortly we move on next to the weaknesses as perceived by the management team, more enthusiasm grows for taking on India. There is a certain amount of perversity in human nature that looking at strengths convinces people about the weakness of their position, but looking at weaknesses forces them to feel more bullish and confident.

Nevertheless, it is important to extract from the general strengths above what might be applicable for the Indian market. It is a way of understanding the real strengths. The following bullet points are an example of that short list:

- Market growth rates
- The company's expertise
- Relationships with suppliers and customers
- Reputation
- Values
- Communication with all stake holders
- Cash generative

This provides a solid base for the next step which is still focused on strengths.

Having tried to relate the strengths that have been perceived in the company very closely to whether they are strengths when entering the Indian market and assembled them in some sort of logical order, it is important to appreciate the diversity of the strengths rather than to suggest that some of them are more important than others. Some of the value of this exercise is in the process as well as the outputs, and if you try to work through this process yourself on your own, remember that what you are looking for at this stage is diversity of thought not some coherence. It is more of a brainstorming than a search after logical truth.

For example in the list above some are focused on qualities of the company, some on India, some on how the company operates.

We then move on to the weaknesses that are perceived, again not stressing any particular perspective for the weaknesses to be grouped around. Most of the answers to this question are pretty similar and are generally focused on lack of knowledge, lack of awareness of a very different business culture, and a general level of ignorance about India. The value in this part of the SWOT is the next stage where I focus on what it is about any particular company that means that these are real weaknesses that cannot be erased by more market research, more in-depth analysis and more information. Again there are no right or wrong answers only perceptions that are more consciously realised and that gives a good insight into the capacity of the company to overcome the weaknesses that are identified. Most importantly it starts to build in my mind at least, and generally in the mind of the participants, an answer to the question of whether the company is ready to enter the Indian market.

I think trying this part of the process out on your own is very hard. I have asked various people over the years to try to do so, just to see whether it can work or whether it needs the group dynamics. The answer is that in general it does need the group, although it is possible to outline the issues working on your own. It is very difficult to get to grips with the weaknesses without the stimulus of other people and other ideas.

In one particularly thoughtful case, where it was part of a senior management team discussion and engagement with the issues, one particular weakness was identified. The precise weakness was that they did not have any back office processes or procedures to deal with an Indian environment. Since this was a company that already had operations overseas, this was quite an admission. As became clearer later, it was a very telling insight into how the company thought of itself. They had entered a second western country's market and taking this as a test bed for a possible move into India showed them that they really needed these back office procedures specifically for the additional country. Even taking a western country where there was a greater commonality of understanding of business and how it is conducted, there were real difficulties for the company in this area. It was an important insight and when we began developing the business case, we had to examine this area in detail. Up until the point where this came out, there was not a shared understanding at all, and the SWOT process had been very useful in identifying this.

A rather typical set of weaknesses can be seen in the following example, which is compiled from several such lists but mainly from the same occasion as the strengths:

- Lack of experience in the market
- Scale of the opportunity and relative size of risk to the company
- Cultural awareness
- Lack of relationships within India
- Lack of reputation within India
- No Intellectual Property established in the market
- Lack of resources within India
- Difficulties of attracting the right staff without the company having a reputation in India
- Back office business model may not be appropriate
- Public relations issues: developing a strategy in India
- And outside of the company itself:
  - o Distribution
  - o Tariffs
  - o Non tariff barriers
  - o Lack of regulatory knowledge
  - o Corruption
  - o Bureaucracy
  - o Terms of payments
- Corruption

The whole basis of these first two parts of the SWOT is to identify the strengths in order to build on them and to isolate the weaknesses so we can eliminate them. It also has the function of building a common purpose. That common purpose does not presuppose a common or agreed answer by any means. In fact it is essential to maintain an understanding that the answer of whether India is right for any particular company at any particular time cannot be answered without going through the whole process.

It is important to apply the same filter to weaknesses as we used on the strengths and to try to come up with the ones that are relevant to the question in hand. The following is an attempt to do this to the list above:

- Lack of relationships
- Lack of reputation
- Distribution
- Finding ways through the bureaucracy
- Lack of experience
- Lack of back office processes appropriate to this new venture
- Corruption
- Attracting the right staff
- Lack of resources
- Cultural awareness and issues
- Terms of payment

The key to understanding how confidence starts to build by considering the weaknesses is perhaps in the way that each of these weaknesses looks readily addressable. Apart from corruption and terms of payment, which may be a bugbear in most developing economies and not amenable to much direct alteration, the rest look solvable by intelligent people taking the appropriate time and advice and formal steps.

With the strengths and weaknesses exposed and not necessarily agreed, and having discovered that the consideration of the weaknesses actually encourages a more optimistic view of the Indian market, I have found that the best way to deal with the opportunities is a round table discussion as opposed to starting by asking people to draw up their own, individual list.

I have tried it other ways and there is a need to judge the individuals within your team in coming to the right approach, but you will probably soon discover what is right for your team. I do have some ends in mind as we go through this part of the process because it is important that people go back to the strengths that have been identified in order to give some meaning to the opportunities. Most people find this challenging, but I want people to focus on the core qualities in their company in order to understand the full range of opportunities. It is not that we will lack focus in the end, only that at this stage, we need to have the right balance between being creative and being focused on the particular issues for a specific company.

The opportunities will obviously be outside much of your company's control and even what the company does now, but crucially they will not be entirely foreign to you. For example, it is much more than the fact that the opportunities are related to the size of a developing market, the low cost and high barriers to entry. Opportunities, especially where India is concerned, are so wide that it is essential to approach them with an open mind. The really important part of the process is the discussion and letting people spread their mental boundaries as they do so. It is not always a successful process, but the best results come from the interplay between members of the team as they start to tease out what the real opportunities are. It is important as this will to some extent create a sense of priorities.

Out of the debate on one occasion came the following:

- Relationships with customers coming from India
- Relationships with customers going to India
- Professional bodies
- Helping customers avoid litigation threats
- Unions being able to pressurise government and companies
- Relationship with governments — Union and State
- Support from suppliers wishing to penetrate the Indian market
- Support from suppliers who already manufacture in India
- Ability to innovate offshore
- Leverage of the brand
- Market innovation
- Reverse engineering — taking back to the UK what we learn or develop in India
- Outsourcing internal business processing
- Staff development
- Shaping the market
- Raising the barriers to competitors
- Corporate Social Responsibility

- Health and Safety commitment
- World citizen
- Growth of the market
- First mover
- Spring board to SE Asia — for example

What I find still inspiring years later about this list is the breadth of thought and even if I do not pretend really to understand all the items, especially the first two in the way they were obviously meant at the time, it is a thought-provoking list. You can also see the value of creativity in identifying being able to take back to the home market what was learnt in India as an opportunity.

For me the most important opportunity was *Shaping the market*. This was important as an opportunity in its own right — and who would turn down such an opportunity — but it was also, more significantly for me than for anyone else in the team, indicative of a developing mind set.

We prioritised the following from this list as likely to be most advantageous to the company:

- Innovation and applying lessons at home
- Support from suppliers
- First mover
- Growth of the market
- Ability to shape the market

What was really encouraging about this prioritised list was that it sounded like the sort of opportunities you would be daft not to grasp. The best contrast is with some of the prosaic answers that are generated about ordinary business opportunities in the West.

I well remember, for example, one corporate grind through a SWOT throwing up the fact that we could grow to 50 million dollars. It does not actually matter if that was a lot or a small amount in this particular context. It just does not grab anyone and make the blood course through their veins.

Following the brain-storming through the opportunities, I have a number of strategies to make the threats section work better.

The first is starting it after a significant break. Lunch works well — and you will probably find the timing for the previous sessions can be adjusted for this very easily.

The second is that people need to be able to focus on the problems and to forget what we have done already, so I have a short session throwing a few ideas around about what the likely types of threat are, almost the only time that I intervene as opposed to facilitate. My examples tend to be rather off the wall and provocative, and deliberately so. One that I throw in has to be used circumspectly, depending upon the audience. It needs a very confident group of people to be told that the company has not got the staying power to go through the inevitable pain barrier. Sometimes I have to dress it up as a wry joke; sometimes I cannot use it at all.

This session is very short and only takes about five minutes.

Then I ask people to work on their own identifying not only the threats — it should be easy to think of more than five with some of the stimulus I give — but then sorting them into some sort of priority or seriousness.

It may be necessary at this point to remind you that we are creating the bedrock on top of which the real planning can be built. However rudimentary the ideas are and however odd the threats seem, they will be real threats to the people who think of them, and they will need to be mitigated, if they cannot be eliminated, in order to create the business case and business plan.

The type of threats that people identify are varied, and that is part of the value of the exercise. Here are some real examples culled from various exercises like this but mainly from the session I am using throughout this discussion:

- Political instability
- Economic downturn potential
- Currency rates/risks
- Trade barriers
- Social unrest
- Lack of timeliness and speed to market
- Pre-emption by another company taking the first move into the market
- Running out of money because costs and time scales underestimated

- IPR issues
- Attracting staff
- Staff retention
- Management time spent on a comparatively small initial business
- Small margins that can be achieved
- Product sourcing
- Suppliers in India plagiarising the approach and brand values
- Bureaucratic delays
- Business declining at home because so much management time devoted to India: an example of opportunity cost
- Inability to establish core values in the Indian company

The prioritised list looked like this:

- Political instability
- Timeliness and speed to market
- Margins that can be achieved
- Other companies getting there first
- Attracting and retaining staff
- Running out of money
- Management time required

Apart from the first one, much of the inherent threat in each of these can be mitigated, if not eliminated, by planning and action. That first one is quite a threat, however. As we have seen, India is not without its political issues and it is as well to recognise this and choose one's destination with that in mind.

At this point I take the temperature of the workshop and assess what people feel. In general there is usually a sense of bewilderment. This sounds the very opposite of building a firm foundation, but we have usually achieved a great deal towards that end.

We have some idea of what threats there are and which ones we can do something about and which ones are beyond our control. We know what we think the weaknesses are. We have a sense of the opportunities and the strengths that can be deployed. What is lacking is some way of establishing the validity of any of the separate points.

That is really how I usually finish off the first day, and what I think you should do at this point. You might not have the range of knowledge and experience of India, but you will have a good business sense of whether you can deploy the strengths you have identified, whether you can grasp the opportunities and whether the threats and the weaknesses mean that you have only a thin level of confidence.

The next stage works very much like a programme for action or even an itinerary. Developing the business case and business plan frameworks actually as a by product point up all the things you do not know. That realisation will give you some sense of the scale of the task.

The business case is the document or presentation that will enthuse the board and sanction the investment. We see a business plan as covering all the hard decisions about establishing a business in India. The business case is derived from the business plan, of course, and this is the order that we use.

As I implied at the beginning of this chapter, this is a voyage of discovery, and much of what you discover as you develop these will be focused on how little you know for certain.

Notice that here we still have not decided the format of how to enter India. I have been through this on many occasions and I have come to the conclusion that there is no really correct answer to the order that is best. My only justification for my rather pragmatic solution is to draw an analogy with developing a partnership or a joint venture. The tendency when doing either is to focus on getting the structure and framework of the partnership absolutely right with all the legal details nailed down. Suddenly you discover that somehow or other six months has passed and you have not actually done anything positive in the way of business.

I prefer to get the ideas moving in people's heads and then worry about the niceties.

The first framework that we address is the business plan. In many ways this is relatively straightforward, but what we produce is a framework not the business plan itself. All the time I stress that people should keep in mind what they discovered about their company from producing the SWOT.

The stages that we go through are the following and we have found the order is significant:

- Identify the products and services that you will propose to sell in India
- Outline the organisation that you will need to develop, support and grow your business, and this includes, where possible, names of real people if you have the right ones
- Understand the requirements for marketing and sales
- Look at issues like distribution and fulfilment
- Think seriously about the professional issues, like registering the company, buying real estate or renting premises

There is a separate heading which I also keep as a series of notes and this is for the assumptions that we are making as we go through the process. As experience alters your perspective, your assumptions will change and it is good to keep the assumptions in your mind and fresh. Those assumptions will be extremely valuable to any independent person examining your business plan, because they are what can be reviewed at a later date and checked for consistency and for validity. Most of your propositions will be too specific and too much derived from the workshop to be readily analysed and appreciated by a third party.

We start with the products and services because that is where most people feel most comfortable and where most companies have usually understood themselves best. I mean by this that there are guidelines or rules of thumb that dictate what sort of product and services mix you will need. I worked with one company, for example, that had an established rule that no customer should ever represent more than 1% of the revenue base. If you think of things in this way you start to understand two key elements that are intrinsic in this discussion:

- How wide a range of products you need
- How wide a range of customers you need

This is of crucial importance, because every different customer segment that you address will add complication to your product set, your organisation and your sales and marketing efforts. Secondly, every extra range of products that you bring to market will also have the same complicating effect. The result may be that you have to re-examine the sort of rules and guidelines that you take for granted in the West before going to India.

Nevertheless, if you look at the initial question, it may seem like a real problem to answer at this point, as there is not much you can say that is open to logical objection about what you may or may not want to sell in India. I mean by that if you suggest that you are going to sell only five products, there is no real way of testing whether this is a good decision or not. This does not matter too much, although it does make some teams uneasy. The point is that whatever you come up with is open to later amendment and it is a good starting point.

To cut through any muddle and to make progress, identify the segments of the market you are going to address and fairly quickly you will see your way through. To make this clear, here is an example. If you are going to address the construction market, you will know which of your products you will be able to deploy, and you will also probably know how wide a product range you need to have an attractive and worthwhile offering.

There are some general questions that you might find useful to ask yourself at this point in order to make progress. I suggest you consider these and then alter or extend the questions to take into account your own special needs:

- Which particular Foreign Direct Investors (FDIs) into the Indian domestic market are creating the largest head count of employees
- Are FDIs banding together to purchase supplies
- How many FDIs are managed by expatriates and which are the ones that are
- Where the main effects of any Corporate Social Responsibility (CSR) pressures are focused
- Where any regulatory bodies are focused
- The numbers of people employed in any particular market sector
- Where the clusters of particular sectors are

- Where the highest growth rates are
- Where the best margins are possible
- What can we source in India either from our existing suppliers who are sourcing in India or from new suppliers?

The antepenultimate question is very important, because, as we have discussed, India's regions and states do have different concentrations of industry that you might be focused on.

Another way of limiting the types of products that you might consider offering in the Indian market is to think about these considerations:

- Service expectations for any particular products
- Competition in your domestic market that might have ensured that you have extremely attractive pricing which might be ideal for India
- Given your company's position with regard to your suppliers and whether developing further revenues in India might improve that relationship by having lower prices for higher volumes, are there any products that would be especially beneficial to you in those terms?

In developing the product offer you will also need to consider the standard questions in your domestic market:

- What do you want to be famous for in India?
- Are you in volume or premium products and services — or both?
- Is providing low cost goods the best way for you to create market entry — by which I mean will you be comfortable with the resulting market position?
- To what extent can you leverage the support or influence of any branded suppliers to you in your home market that also have a presence in India?
- Do specific brands have a value in the market already?
- To what extent should you be opportunistic and to what extent focus on delivering your strategic focus?
- Can you use any value engineering approach to create a better offer?

There are further questions, such as are you prepared to work on a consignment basis, but you will have the idea now of how to focus on what you would be comfortable doing in the Indian market.

The only proviso that I would add is to ensure you ask yourself whether this is an initial position or one that you will want to change over time.

The next clear issue in any business plan is the type of organisation you will be comfortable using. Here the answers will be a good deal easier to arrive at, as India has pretty well every permutation of organisation that you could wish for. What you need to understand is how you will achieve the most flexible organisation that you as a company are comfortable with.

I look at the types of company that you might consider creating in the next chapter so I am not too concerned about that here. It is such a big subject that I did not want to treat it too quickly but examine in detail the pros and cons of each approach.

In outline you will need to have a view on the following considerations:

- How much of the management can actually still be done from your home headquarters?
- Do you want to appoint an expatriate managing director — with a brief to recruit and train his or her successor or will you start with an Indian senior manager?
- What focus — other than creating the business and generating a return over a specific number of years — will you direct the senior manager with? For example, will you want to create a reputation for thought leadership or value for money or premium products — or any combination of such points?
- Will you need a product manager in India and if so how will you ensure that the person is inducted into the business properly and has all your values and then has all the appropriate training?
- Will you expect a product manager to be responsible for marketing, so can you double up that responsibility or will you use your home marketing person or people?
- Depending upon the anticipated number of products and what sort of range of customers you will be targeting, how many sales people will you

need — taking, from my experience of start ups in India, one sales manager for each four sales people?

- What sort of back office will you need in India — if any — and what sort of logistics and what will this translate into in terms of full time equivalents?
- Will you need a customer service manager?
- Will you need a finance head or a bookkeeper — or can those functions be initially run from home?

As you can see, this is not that different from establishing a new business in a new region to you at home, and you will be able to work on rough assumptions here. Obviously, to my way of thinking, do take a worst case scenario of costs involved.

There is a difference, however, as the sheer distance and, for example, time zones between your home country and India will mean that you have to anticipate that it will be more difficult. For example, in your home market or setting up in an adjacent country, you might well be able to piggy back on the technical knowledge of your products in head office and save costs and training time in the new business. In India this is likely to be more challenging and, at the very least, you will need to have a process written to ensure it happens effectively.

It is all very well for me to suggest that writing up the processes and really looking at your procedures and policies is of long term benefit to your company but there is the reality that this is an extra burden and you will find it hard to make the time to do it. On the other hand, as I suggested in an earlier chapter, this is a short term hidden cost, but a long term hidden benefit.

Let me pose one or two further questions that will give further insights into the tricky issues that you need to have right.

Can you use your IT systems in headquarters in India? With the type of communications that we can cheaply tap into now, this is not the unlikely scenario that it would have been even as little as five years ago. Many of our clients for business processing give us access from India into their systems, saving a whole degree of duplication. On the other hand, it takes some planning and thought, and extra focus on security.

Do you think your human resources department would be able to cope with new employees in India? I do not know if it is strange or not, and it is certainly unexpected for me, but in general western human resources departments cope with the oddities of India almost better than any other company department. I am told it is because they focus on the human, on the common factors, but my experience of human resources departments tends to make me sceptical of this.

Can your procurement people deal with issues at long range? Unlike the human resources people, procurement nearly always makes heavy weather of India. I have my theories there, which you will have seen in earlier chapters, but here just note it as a fact.

Will the company secretary be comfortable with a different legal environment which might look and act the same, but which has enough different twists to keep you awake at night?

On the other hand, there is also the opposite benefit, hinted at before, of being able to use Indian resources in your home country. For example, after what may be a short time, you might well be able to move a substantial part of your back office processing to your Indian concern.

I would seriously advise you not to make this part of your business plan, if only because finance directors for one tend to view this sceptically and it appears to weaken the argument if you have to drag in such a point to make the business plan and in turn the business case fly. Nevertheless, you might find it something useful to keep up your sleeve as an additional benefit after the business plan and case have in large part been accepted.

Look too at the benefits if employees can move from one location to another, with the cross fertilisation of expertise and experience initially benefiting the Indian operation and the fresh pair of eyes benefiting your home operations in due course. Then in the longer term you will find that you have probably stimulated a freer movement of ideas between the two organisations and both will benefit from the different perspectives.

Having created a warmer glow from these possibilities, do remember the training requirement and in all seriousness, do add quite a contingency into any training plans you might already have. In many ways it is prudent to double the usual training time you allow in your home country, not because your Indian staff will be less bright or adaptable than your existing staff, only that they will lack familiarity with ordinary ways of working that you do not even notice but which will be very strange to your Indian staff.

You should also ensure that you modify — or create — an induction plan and that this is suitably realistic too, by which I mean if it takes two days in your home market, make it five in India.

You may also have some inbuilt costs in just the way you do things and you will have to take a decision whether you will perpetuate those accepted practices in India. How will you treat sickness and pensions in India — the way you do in the West, which is partly caused by legislation and regulation but is now more or less an accepted cost of doing business — or differently? You will not absolutely need to bear these costs in India, but you might think it appropriate to do so.

Finally, you will need to add to the costs of creating your organisation in India the costs of expanding, either within one region or in two or more, and then going national. There are no right answers, but experience shows that if you can successfully launch a business in one area, as long as the essential pre-conditions are there, for example, the type of customers, you will be able to move on and up pretty quickly elsewhere in India.

Marketing and sales are pretty well covered in the organisation in terms of numbers, but this is more focused on what sort of marketing you want to use. This comes back to those fundamental marketing questions that we are all used to in our home markets. Take for example the one I naturally focus on: do we need to use broadcasting or narrowcasting methods. In short, is our target customer base a mass market or a small, defined number of companies — or somewhere in between.

The change in India that I have most noticed in this respect over the last two years has been the move to more and more Internet-based marketing and, in turn, sales. You will know your market and this will give you the scale of costs that you will be interested in for creating the business case.

Distribution and how you effect it will also be a larger cost in India than it is in your home market. The only way adequately to consider distribution costs is to think that in India the cost of fuel before tax is at least equivalent to your home experience, and it is a relatively high expense. The cost of cars and trucks is about the same, but labour is cheaper. On the other hand, everything will take twice as long, at least. In short, as a rule of thumb, double your logistics costs.

Then you have the costs for all of the professional services, such as accountants, lawyers and estate agents or realtors.

If you are used to paying £450 or $900 per hour for a tax advisor from your accountants — that is not to say comfortable with that level of fee — then you are in for a pleasant surprise in India, but, on the other hand, everything does take that much longer and there is always a range of incidental charges.

Putting your costs together will create your outline business case, but it is at this point just that: an outline business case. If it is possible, this is the time to plan your trip to India as a fact finding mission. It probably would not be your first trip, but it is important to go at this stage. It is not to prove your assumptions in the business case, it is to test them.

As you take the trip, be doubly aware of the hidden costs that we have looked at; treat every *yes* with circumspection. You will find that you can establish a great deal in five days if you plan it right, start at about 9.30 am every morning and expect to finish gone eleven — at night.

On your return, you will be able to check your assumptions and create a reasonably accurate business case to put before the board. Of course this is also the moment when you look back at all those strengths and if you have majored on the *can do attitude* that you are convinced your company has, you may start to have doubts. You will be so aware of the range of issues, but most people are also aware at this point of the opportunities that beckon.

Prior to presenting the business case, you need to re-check the business plan. You will then re-assess your assumptions and produce a final draft of the business case.

The business plan will have one major plank missing at this point — the one that I cover in the next chapter. It will lack the actual structure of the company you will establish, whether it be greenfield, an acquisition, a joint venture with an established company, a joint venture with a partner new to some aspects of what you are doing, a distributor arrangement, some form of franchise, or some form of arrangement usually dignified by a four letter acronym: *DBOT*. Design, build, operate — and transfer. I add the hyphen and the space after operate, as transfer usually takes a very long time.

Once you do understand the nature of the company you will be building you can add that to the business plan and update the business case.

The next essential elements to the plan are reasonably straightforward:

- Location — if there are going to be two or more
- Number of locations — if there are going to be two or more
- Time scales for establishing each
- Time from first setting up, in however limited a way, to actual trading
- Time to local sourcing — however limited
- Time to having the most senior manager an Indian
- Time to being cash positive
- Time to being profitable
- Return on investment (ROI)

The latter two, of course, are more likely to be seen as part of the business case, but when you are thinking of setting up in India I would leave the consideration of these two till now.

Location will be determined, I suggest, by knowledge of which industries are where in India, which tax regimes are most beneficial for you, the availability and relevance of special economic zones (SEZs), any local knowledge you or your advisers have, and a careful selection of going either where all your competitors already are or choosing to steer clear of your known competitors.

I am not making light of this consideration, and you should take a serious amount of research into account for this.

In terms of location, I sometimes wonder whether my prejudices about places in India come into my preferences for particular clients, but I think not. It is quite difficult to like, positively like, Mumbai, but there is no doubt that it has plenty of reasons for being a good first location.

The number of locations that you will plan on having is also crucial. In many ways I do think it is a good idea to have the number in mind. Once you get to three metros or locations in India, you will start to feel that you can address India properly whereas one location will always feel like a bit of a sideshow, even if it is in, say, Delhi.

Time to first trading is really the first sense of a target for most people — far more than the point of setting up. Whatever you do, avoid too much optimism even in your pragmatic, sensible mind on this.

Local sourcing is something that will be very difficult to predict, but if you tie it in with the idea of having the most senior manager being Indian, you will probably know what your company will be able to achieve. (This is a business culture matter as much as a question of individual personalities.)

Time to be cash positive through to being profitable will concentrate the mind, as it always will, whether you are in Boise or Frankfurt, Reading or Fort Worth.

As I said at the outset of this chapter, what we have here is a framework. There is always some scepticism before we start this process whether we can achieve anything worthwhile in two or three days, but the process we go through is very productive, and the great thing about it, as we have shown over many iterations, is that it is very flexible.

Almost flexible enough for India.

EIGHT

HOW TO ENTER THE MARKET: PARTNERSHIP, DISTRIBUTORSHIP, JOINT VENTURE, DBOT, OR DO IT YOURSELF

I n what seems like a paradox when you first encounter it, and before I look at the type of company you might start in India, there are one or two important issues that I want to draw immediate attention to.

I always start any discussion about starting up a new venture with how to get out of it. If you are thinking about entering the Indian market in a joint venture or in a partnership or some other relationship with an Indian company, this should figure high in your considerations. This is not some semantic nicety but the result of experience and, in one instance, bitter experience. By giving the example, I hope to underline how important the exit strategy is right at the beginning of a relationship.

A large financial services company that I knew had got into terrible trouble in an outsourcing deal. For both sides it had proved unsustainable with, probably, false expectations created at the beginning. The whole juggernaut — it was a massive deal — had got to the point where both sides wanted out, but there was no proper exit strategy in the original contract. In one real sense, that was not a problem because they were going to get expensive lawyers on both sides to achieve the divorce. And there was the clue. It was like the end of a relationship and what they had was a lot of loose ends.

There was, for example, no agreement readily arrived at on who owned the hardware. Of course the hardware that had existed prior to the agreement was the company's, but no one was prepared to consider what was supposed to happen to the hardware bought since. This was, however, the tip of the iceberg. Software had been developed by the supplier in order to achieve cost savings in the way the contract was run. Who owned it? What was a fair price for its development — and then who owned the intellectual property rights in a substantial piece of software that was deliberately designed to be used by the supplier on more than one contract?

New working practices had been developed at considerable cost. Were they just part of the deal or were they something which had a value when being transferred back? The staff themselves, since this was in Europe, were also another issue because the staff's terms and conditions and working practices were all tied up in TUPE — transfer of undertaking, protection of employment legislation. I have been involved in many TUPE issues — some where we could have had as many opinions as we were prepared to pay lawyers because it is so full of grey areas — but this one looked straightforward, and was not.

If we go back to that *divorce* for a moment, you can see the parallel: a prenuptial agreement. If you think how bitter some divorces can be even with a prenuptial agreement — whether or not recognised by the jurisdiction that the divorce is fought out under — you will have some idea of how important it is to focus on the exit.

Nearly all the items identified above, apart from TUPE, are likely to be considerations in any exit clauses if you intend to create a partnership, joint venture or even a distributorship model in India. Over the years, having been involved in creating quite a few of these, I have discovered another use for getting the exit clause — or prenuptial agreement — fixed before you do anything more. The way I get to the heart of what has to be in the exit clause seems quite laborious, but what it does expose almost better than anything else is what people actually want out of the contractual agreement.

I conduct a workshop or a brainstorm session, with no right answers, with each side in turn. I deliberately leave out one instruction that I insert later in the process.

I start with the simple questions, *what do you imagine would precipitate you wanting to get out of this agreement?* The answers to this are pretty standard and most of us can predict them:

- Discovery of fraud or some other malpractice
- Failure by the other party to deliver the terms of the agreement
- A change in their management and their focus
- A bad clash over policy or process
- Some sort of ethical issue
- A realisation that this was not the right thing to do

I then push pretty hard on this and try to take them through separate scenarios partly to remove the focus on the other party getting things wrong, which is the natural bent of most answers. I say it is natural because most people with good intentions will not be conscious of not delivering their side of the bargain.

I ask:

- What happens if a better opportunity comes along?
- What happens if the economic situation changes?
- What happens if you find that their approach to staffing is unacceptable to you?
- What happens if you discover that the benefits are substantially weighted more to them than to you?
- What happens if you realise that it just can not work out — through no fault on either side but just sheer bad luck that you have chosen to do the wrong thing with the wrong second party?

The point that I reinsert into the argument here — and I have been moving each side separately towards it — is the fact that these will generate reciprocal clauses. If you want the opportunity to exit just because you do not like the other side, then the other party has to have that same option. How would you feel if you were twenty four months into a contract and the other party was able to pull out on just a whim?

You can see this is just a very difficult balancing act. All of this is not difficult to resolve — it just takes realism and a focus on something that you would rather not be contemplating.

There is a final stage to the interrogation before I get on to the difficult issues, and this is to ask whether there is anything else that might trigger an exit.

Up until this point, I have rarely had any surprises when working through the issues. Very often I will not get a response to this question until a following day or even later than that, because this is extraordinarily difficult to work through. I ask them to consult their colleagues and anyone else they know who has got into a joint venture or partnership or other contractual issue entering a new market.

The issue that comes up here — as I say it might be eventually — is what control actually means. Within your own organisation or company you will have been used to exercising control in a way that you will not be able to do if you enter this sort of contractual obligation. The real question that needs to be asked is at which point will you cease being comfortable if, for example, the other side has the final say. Articulating this precisely is very difficult, and I have to use examples that are pertinent to the situation to make sure that people are able to deal with this objectively.

Ask yourself something like the following and decide how you would want to deal with it:

- The new entity has been trading for six months and established a reasonable position though it is not yet profitable. You want to expand immediately and the other side wants to wait until the trading position is absolutely certain — how are you going to resolve this?

- The new entity has been trading for six months and not yet achieved any of its milestones and you want to make changes that the other side says are premature — how are you going to resolve this?

If you believe you are right and the other side says that you are being premature, control — and this is not the contractual control but the real power in the way the new company is going to develop — is clearly the issue. Imagine that the other side is, in their opinion, *firm* and in your opinion *obstinate* — which are two sides of the same concept — what do both sides do to resolve the problem?

In many ways the scenarios that I have painted above must seem obvious, but I have to say that there is usually a process before we get to this point. The great thing about this is that it often does something that I have not been able to achieve in any other way: it reveals to the people concerned what they are really interested in and where their breaking points are. I may be able to characterise it as a focus on power, but it is often deeper than that, not easily reconcilable and takes any number of forms.

If I take an example that seems outside of this at first, you will see what I mean. Nagging away at the managing director one time during the process described above was something he could not put his finger on. He then worked through several particular issues and together we worked out that none of the examples I was giving him gave him any trouble. He was relaxed about operational decisions of the type where the entity has to expand or consolidate. His point of sensitivity was over how he knew the figures were right. Expressed in its simplest form he needed the finance office or the new company to be his appointee. You can see that is a control issue, but it did not appear like this to him until he got to the end of the process.

Once we have all these issues out in the open, they are merely contractual issues that can be satisfied with a form of words one way or another. On the other hand, do not underestimate that teasing them out can be difficult.

The next step in this worst case analysis is to divide the spoils. As I said above, please focus not only on the tangibles, like hardware and software and the stock that the company has created or bought, but look seriously at the intangibles, such as brand strength and reputation.

Remember that this is reciprocal and try to see how the separation of assets can be a two-edged sword. For example, you may have created a successful model for going to market but just each have the wrong partner. If you have created a business plan together, will you be comfortable letting the other side have it? Will they be comfortable letting you have all the benefit? Would it be a problem if both sides, having split for whatever reason, then wanted to implement the same process again with new partners or on their own?

It is vital to keep in mind that either or both of you may well want to try again even following a failure that we are not predicting but anticipating. It is, after all, highly likely that one of you will want to try again in some form or other.

There is a two stage process here which is common to all such arrangements:

- Understand what intellectual property you brought to the new company and understand what new intellectual property you will create, either separately or together, in the new company.
- Have a clear plan for dividing it up, having worked out what you might want to do following any break up.

In short — think the unthinkable and think it through to the bitter end.

You may find this very difficult to raise as a subject but you can always encourage your advisers, whether they are consultants, lawyers or accountants, to initiate the discussion.

If this has not daunted you too much — and it should be a good deal less daunting than actually having to implement it or even face a separation without such a plan — you need to build one further safeguard into any contractual obligations you may enter into dealing with India. You have to ensure that whatever else, you can go to independent arbitration, preferably in your home jurisdiction, although this can be quite impossible to achieve and sometimes a nonsense in practice.

I have suggested, on good evidence, that it is possible to go to court in India to enforce your contract and to have it resolved in a reasonably short time. My advice is, however, that this ought to be considered the exception not the rule. I was once told by a barrister in the UK that going to court should always be the last option of anyone who has their wits about them. In India, the advice must be to avoid any legal action like the plague. There are perfectly good ways of having arbitration written into your contracts in India and I think it is vital.

If you take these two points seriously, working out your exit strategy and building in arbitration, I can not guarantee that you will be successful, but I can guarantee that failure will be a good deal less painful that it might be. As a pessimistic business planner myself, I prefer that sense of disaster mitigated.

There is one other essential element already mentioned that you just have to be aware of but putting appropriate safeguards in place will tax the most imaginative lawyer and probably your own understanding of people. That is protecting your intellectual property. There are laws in India that appear to safeguard your position. I do not think there is any substitute for wariness and trusting your own judgement about anyone you are dealing with.

Think very carefully about how precious the information you are giving access to is to you, your business and to other people. If it is too valuable to lose, it might be too valuable to use in India for the time being. In some ways this is no different from anywhere else in the world, but reading people across a cultural divide is so tricky that you have to be doubly anxious.

Having sorted out key elements in the nuts and bolts, it is a good idea to have a look at the whole engine. There are all sorts of ways of entering the Indian market. I have come to the conclusion that the one that looks the most daunting is actually the one that makes most sense to most companies and is probably the most effective. I have listened to many other people who have informed opinions on this and I cannot say I am a minority of one, but you will probably find as many opinions as there are informed people.

I suppose my answer has been created in the full glare of costs and time running away.

There are essentially six ways of entering the Indian market which actually become five when you start looking at the difficulties:

- Create a joint venture
- Create some form of partnership
- Take over a company in India
- Ask a supplier to design, build and operate a company for you with an eye on transferring it to you eventually — this is usually known as DBOT
- Find one or more distributors
- Start from scratch on your own account

These approaches apply whether your business is B2B or B2C. There are more compelling arguments for some sort of distributor relationship or joint venture if your business model is B2C, and I do not discount that in the discussion below. In that sort of model, distribution is so much more important than many other considerations, and that is the value that a joint venture or, more particularly, using a distributor can bring.

Let me apply the usual word of warning about time considerations in India. In understanding the paragraphs below, start by appreciating the quantity of work that will be required and the time it would take in a western country other than your own and add on at least 50% to allow for the special qualities that India demands.

I have discussed starting from scratch with a number of B2C companies. Not one has actually gone it alone, but some have come close to taking that route. The apparent investment upfront has been the decider in each case. I think the jury is out, but I can not really argue with the pragmatic approach I have seen adopted.

My mainstream discussion below is centered on B2B, where I have seen a range of approaches. I do not think for one moment that there is just one correct way, but my favoured way is to start from scratch on your own account. That does not mean I rule out the other ones, and I will start by looking at the pros and cons of each of the options above. You might detect some inherent bias in my approach, which is why I made sure that

I identified my favoured approach first. You can allow for my assumptions being based on that favoured approach.

The difference between the first two methods of entering the Indian market, creating a joint venture or creating some form of partnership, is one, essentially, of formality. The same issues and the same benefits arise from each. That is why I think we can take them together.

The undoubted benefits of a joint venture or a partnership are mainly derived from the local insights the other party will have. You will no doubt be dealing with a reasonably successful business in India that you wish to enter into some sort of arrangement with. To be successful, the other company will have had to establish a business, register it, work out all the costings — or at least be able to assemble the costs from the process they have been through, create a marketing and sales plan, create a logistics channel, and in general anticipate all the pain. They will have used every professional service you will need and will have a good or at least serviceable network of contacts.

You will be able to find a large number of companies that are of sufficient size to be of interest, whatever the size of your company, and there is an appetite in India for these joint ventures. It is not an altruistic interest, which means that it is more reliable. Your potential Indian partner will be looking to learn from the joint venture as well as create any value or profit from it. Remember my advice above about your intellectual property and that protecting it will be extraordinarily difficult. It may be that the ideas involved are pretty low level and nothing to worry about. They can still be valuable in India and no threat to your business elsewhere. If you think that you could earn good money from your consultancy on your intellectual property and how you do things, it is probably valuable enough to protect and to be concerned about sharing it.

The main problems you will face with a joint venture or a partner will not initially be in this area. It will be in just understanding or working out who you are dealing with.

Ownership, even of public companies, can be a nightmare to disentangle in India. You will find cross holdings, holdings inside a family that are rather unreliably reported, and all sorts of share holdings that are not quite what they seem. A reasonably well known company in the IT space, for example, is more or less accurately deniably related to another with which I have known it apparently to be in competition. At the same time, a sceptic might view the relationship between the two major shareholders of each company as being unquestionably within the family, since they are married to each other.

This would be important anywhere in the world, but within India where the hierarchical structure of companies is so important, and where power and authority is rarely transferred down the chain of command, it becomes vital. You have to know who the real decision maker is, and I have had trouble with this, even when I am aware and wary.

The second issue that I think is really significant, and has been a major determinant in companies not going forward with a joint venture or partnership, is cultural fit between companies. You will have seen enough in this book about the lack of cultural fit between Indian business and western business and how even when well disguised it may come back to haunt you. I am not concerned with that here. I am focusing on the expectations you have about how business is conducted and how an Indian company will expect business to operate. My objection is not in the end that you will not be able to find a company that you can form a joint venture or partnership with, one that has a suitably similar corporate ethos and a sense of propriety that is similar to yours. My objection lies in the amount of time it takes to find that company.

It is not as though there is some form of computer dating where you can tick thirty boxes and the company of your dreams will be introduced to you. There is probably room in the market place for just such a service to be provided but until it is there, it is hit and miss.

If my experience is anything to go by, you will get to a point where that chilling phrase *that'll do for now* raises its head and you will find that you are contemplating forming an important company alliance despite the underlying feeling that you are working with a partner that may well not be the best or even good enough. The search process is very enervating in itself and I think takes you away from the very point of the process, which is getting to know the Indian market and entering it. Serendipity may strike and you may chance on the company or companies that immediately appeal to you, and which find your approach and business proposition equally attractive. I just have not seen it.

My real objection therefore is not that you will not find the right fit but that it will take you too long — and your time can be better spent in other ways. There are a good many examples that I have known — and I have worked on one particular joint venture which did start off with a good deal of luck in apparently finding the right partner — where my pessimism looked initially unfounded, but was entirely appropriate.

It is probably sensible, nevertheless, to offer some insights into creating a partnership with a company in India. This may seem to have a good deal to recommend it as it does not have quite the legal paraphernalia surrounding it and the risk to your company is probably more easily contained. My experience, however, is that partnerships take a good deal of effort to make work, precisely because the legal structure is not there, and there is some sort of casual assumption that good will can carry the venture forwards. It just does not work like that.

Partnership, of course, is one of those words which means whatever the person using it happens to mean at that moment. It is rather ethereal in my experience, unless you take it seriously and put in place some structures to support it. Sustaining a partnership is time consuming and extremely difficult, especially as inbuilt to any such arrangement is asynchronous benefit. One of the partners will inevitably achieve a greater benefit from the arrangement earlier than the other and at that point tensions start. In many cases this greater benefit will in fact be time bound as the other partner will achieve greater benefit later. Nevertheless this can cause instability if it is not recognised up front.

My solution, and it does have real benefits, is to create a process for sustaining the partnership, and while this may seem time consuming it will in due course save a good deal of time and effort. When I explain the approach to clients they almost invariably suggest that it is too much of an investment of senior management time. I counter this by asking them if they have any experience of partnerships, and can they work out how much time is demanded on an ad hoc basis in those arrangements. Even if the time is less than I am proposing for the sustainability processes, the very fact that it is ad hoc makes it disruptive. In any case, most companies have never worked out the time involved, and when they do they are rather surprised and find my approach to partnerships will in fact save time and effort — and produce a more stable partnership. Not much of this is India specific, of course, except that the cross cultural issues mean that a recognised process is even more important.

In some ways there are parallels with establishing a distributorship — and it might be useful to read the section below in conjunction with this.

The same advantages and disadvantages fundamentally apply to buying into or buying a company in India. Due diligence is time consuming and challenging. We use a detective agency and that is reasonably satisfactory in the sense that we have not ever been challenged afterwards because we had missed something. It, being India, is not that expensive. The trouble is, of course, that you do not know what you do not know even at the end of an investigation. We have, however, turned up really disturbing facts about various companies and individuals. Our clients have at first been dismayed by the information as they had established expectations in their own minds about what they were going to do, but then relieved that it was out in the open.

Buying a company obviously has to rely a great deal on what due diligence you can do. My experience of observing a company that was already established in India move towards buying a company in India was salutary. As they had had experience of setting up and creating a business their own insights into what a company should look like and what they should themselves focus on were soundly based. In short I think my advice is to take it at a reasonable pace and establish yourself first before contemplating buying into an established Indian company in India.

The fourth way of establishing yourself in India, used reasonably successfully by outsourcing companies, is to find a supplier to design your operation, build it, operate it — though this is obviously optional — and then transfer it to you. This is known in IT circles as DBOT, pronounced *Deebot*. I have only known of one example where the T got translated into action — that is, the company was *Transferred*. There is a great deal to recommend in this approach particularly with one major caveat. If you ensure that a member of your staff is part of the DBOT activity from the beginning and is embedded in the operation, you will gain maximum benefit. The transfer of knowledge from the supplier to you is probably at least as important as the transfer of the undertaking, if that, indeed, takes place. I say this because you will in all probability want to set up another company in another metro or region of India, and whether you decide to do this on your own or with the same supplier, having those insights will be invaluable.

The main issue that I have found with DBOT is how your supplier costs the whole process and whether you are able to assess if the price is reasonable. As you can imagine it is not particularly easy to isolate all the costs, and even the acquisition of a site, for example, can lead to rather nasty surprises. There is always friction about pricing in these examples, unless the supplier has put too much contingency into the package. My rule of thumb is in fact that if there is no friction over pricing during the life of the process, you are paying over the odds.

On the other hand, because you are effectively at arm's length from the supplier and it is a contractual relationship with relatively tightly defined accountabilities and time scales, there is a good deal to recommend it, not least the slightly lower importance of due diligence. What you need here is references and references that you can check in person and that are related to what you want to do. If the references are with western businesses, this is clearly much more convincing. On balance DBOT would be my second recommendation.

Setting up a distributorship, especially if you are used to using such a channel to market, has a number of advantages. You are effectively outsourcing a good deal of the risk and giving yourself access to a good deal of local knowledge almost immediately. The amount of due diligence you have to do is reasonable and you will be able to see how successful the company is with its current product range more or less by turning up and looking. You can also question the company's customers or clients.

I am just so wary of using a distributor from my own experience of setting one up in India and working with them — or, somehow, against them. The company I was working for already had distributors round the globe and so understood how to work with them. I had been extremely careful in the selection of the potential distributor and there were no problems apparently in that regard. The company was sound, had good sales people, a real understanding of the market that we wanted to enter, and was able to demonstrate a good pedigree in being a distributor. In fact the impetus for them to be a distributor for us had come from their success for a competitor. Our competitor had decided on the back of the success its distributor had had, that the market had been grown so effectively that they had to own the distribution.

Our problem became apparent fairly quickly. It was just that it seemed to take more effort than doing it ourselves to keep them focused, ensure they reported back, and achieve anything at all. We trained the sales and support people — two weeks back in the UK. We did the sales plans and went on some initial sales calls. Collateral provided by us was first class. All in all, while I recognised it was not a straightforward sales process as it was introducing a new type of product into the IT space in India, I became convinced we should just have done it ourselves because that would have taken less effort overall.

I know that I can not generalise from this one example and I am not, as I am taking into account a number of other examples. I know of examples in the West where the same is true so it is not, again, a phenomenon of the Indian market alone. I do know of successful examples, but in every case the effort that had to be put in was reckoned in hindsight to be a good deal more than had been bargained for. It is not that this degree of effort meant that a distributorship was not the right answer, only that the effort should not be underestimated.

You will remember the Indian proclivity for moving on to the next new thing — and that is one of the major stumbling blocks we had with our distributor. Keeping the focus on our product set, especially when the sales cycle proved longer than the Indian company had bargained for, though we had said very precisely what it would be, was very tough.

Of course you will know more about your own requirements and how you need to proceed, but in the end I have usually come to the conclusion that setting up on your own is at least the idea that you have to examine most seriously and if it proves not the best for you, so well and good. At least you will have made an informed decision. I think the next best is the DBOT approach, but it is very early days for anything other than outsourcing, and the levels of experience amongst the professionals who will be involved, the lawyers and accountants and bankers, are low.

The advantages that I usually list for setting up on your own include the following:

- There is a good deal less due diligence to be carried out
- There is less of a concern with matching cultures between companies and with anticipating different approaches and having to compromise in any areas
- Control is not an issue and it certainly is if you take any other route
- Exit is a good deal easier
- You will not put your intellectual property at so great a risk
- You keep the value

If you look at this list and see which considerations are important to you, you will be able to come to a reasonable view about your propensity to go about it alone.

The disadvantages are mostly contained in the advantages I have listed for each method, but they generally boil down to this list:

- You will not have the same local knowledge
- You might be more at the mercy of less fastidious professionals — and they exist in India as elsewhere
- You will need to establish your own network of people, including, potentially, suppliers and customers and consultants
- You will need much, much more guidance through the maze of bureaucracy
- You will need to allow more time than you initially imagine, even after you have added contingency, before you are up and running
- You will have to learn very fast — and you will need your person from your western operations in India

- Recruitment may well be much more difficult than you can bargain for at the beginning of this process

I suppose the list above says it is not easy, but remember my key point that these barriers to entry apply to your western competitors and if you can get into India and establish yourself first, those barriers to entry work in your favour.

I mentioned the professionals above, and if you have not availed your-selves of consultancy in the West to set up in India, these Indian profession-als will be your lifeline. As I have written in earlier chapters, I have met some of the best accountants in the world in India. I have also met as many indif-ferent ones as a normal curve of distribution would suggest.

The key initial criterion that I use for assessing the capabilities of an accountant, after I have used whatever innate but not very trustworthy feel-ings I have, is to ask them how they would go about sorting out all the reg-istrations that are required. If the answer is that they have the usual brother-in-law or cousin strategically placed you are getting to firmer ground. Ask to meet the individual and assess him or her. Whatever else you need from your accountant, he or she has to be well connected at the lower levels of the bureaucracy to make anything work. If you add on half as much again to any time scales that the accountant's brother-in-law gives you and you still have not achieved what was required, think seriously about chang-ing your accountant.

I start with accountants for this rather than lawyers, because accountants make the world go round in India. I suppose the same is true of most coun-tries and business areas, but it is just so much more marked in India because of the special qualities they need to possess. You will remember the example I gave in an earlier chapter.

Lawyers in India are a breed apart. They are faced daily with a legal sys-tem that has had liberal quantities of super glue applied and which is rather despised and avoided by everyone in sight, but which can move — as I have shown earlier — and does move rather unexpectedly. In extreme contrast to the possibility of ever going to court, contracts, as I have said, are puzzled through by lawyers with amazing attention to detail. Days have gone by comparing the results of changing a word. They have to be amazing to work in India, and my experience is that they are. You meet the rogues and the less than competent, but the good lawyers are first class. I do not really have a rule of thumb for assessing them, except to see how realistic they are. Generally reckon their quality in inverse proportion to their confidence of achieving anything quickly.

Bankers can also be your allies in India. Expect the highest standards of probity and you will not be disappointed. You will find the speed, the absent-mindedness of some of the instructions and the high levels of confidence in being able to fulfil actions by a certain date rather challenging, but you will find they come through, although it may be eventually. It is not usually as bad as the Gulf, for instance, where, having been given a list of all the documents that anyone could require to change the signatories on an account, each time I returned I was asked for a further document, but it can happen. Even in India, if you are requested to produce a set of documents to support your application for something, like opening an account, ask for that full list in writing. Get someone, even the door sweeper, to sign off that this is the complete list of documents, and resist all attempts to suggest that in fact there is just one more now required. Intransigence works, eventually, though you may have to concede the first attempt.

You can expect good, pedantic service from banks in India.

Other services that you will need, like realtors or estate agents and public relations companies, will in no small measure reproduce the standards and caricatures that they enjoy in the West. There must be somewhere an overarching policy manual for each of these professions that transcends country cultures and geographical location. Listening to a property professional sucking in breath in shocked amazement at the paltry sum of money you are prepared to offer for what is obviously a gem even though it is set within a mass of detritus, sounds much the same in Noida as it does in Fort Worth or Lyons. Place as much trust in these people as you do at home and you will not go too far wrong.

Outside of India, I have not any experience of using detective agencies. The experience in India really only has one message which is that under no circumstances should you expect to agree to the first quotation that they will give you. Experience has shown that this is probably inflated by about 25% over what they expect to receive. Do also draw up tight terms of reference with your expectations firmly indicated. I doubt that this is different from anywhere else in the world, but it might be a useful insight.

Any general advice on people supplying professional services in India will not be that different from the acid tests that you apply at home. Look for some fact or statement in whatever you are told that you can independently verify. Look for references, although you may well not know how independent the referee will be. Ask for lists of satisfied clients.

The point that most people make to me is that they do not know where to start. I have some obvious answers to that point as we run a consultancy set up to do just that, but experience has also shown that you need to take two trips. The first time you will inevitably be bowled over by India, for good or ill. You will need time to go home and digest what has happened. Whatever you do, do not make any decisions based on that first trip.

Your second trip, at least a month later, will be the valuable one, where you will start to create a frame of reference for what the Indian experience is all about and whether it is for you and whether it offers a real opportunity for your company. That is when I advise you to start talking to the professionals that you might want to use. Before then you will not have enough of a perspective to understand what is really important and what is merely a bubble of excitement or a deep well of gloom.

Perhaps because India is so strange, in that second trip you will start to see part of it as familiar and yet be uncomfortable with that feeling. That is the position I always wanted to aim for in my own mind, contrary and contradictory as it may seem.

On your second trip, you will understand what I mean.

SALES AND MARKETING IN INDIA

I have focused heavily on understanding not only the products and services you will be able to sell in India but on the expertise that you bring, treating that as either a product or service to sell or a key differentiator for you. At this stage in understanding whether you are going to enter the Indian market or not, you have to decide precisely how you are going to bring yourself to market.

My assumption here is that the market we are addressing in India is the growing middle class — however we see fit to define it. This today might be 250 million people, it might be 150 million, it might be 300 million. It might be those with incomes above $5,000 per year, it might be those who speak sufficiently good English. The definition does not matter.

We do know that the number of people who can be counted in that grouping is growing currently at more than 5% per year. We also know that the people entering that category are not divorced from the reality they are in the process of leaving behind, nor are those who are already in a more fortunate position divorced from that reality. They are still Indians, and conscious of being part of an India with major issues, not least grinding poverty for a large number of the population.

The considerations that this should cause you will be part of the succeeding paragraphs, but first we need to look at your company.

For a consultancy of the type I manage, it is second nature to see the value in the knowledge, experience, insights, and skills that we have. It is what we live by. For many companies in the West, however, this is rarely considered in the detail that is essential for India — and actually, I have come to believe, more essential than most people know for their survival and growth in the West.

Whatever that skill, knowledge, experience or insight might be, it, of course, has no value if, first of all, it does not differentiate you in the market place. Whether your consultancy capabilities can differentiate you in India might seem impossible to understand without more knowledge of the market in India. This is true to a point, but you do have an immediate differentiator that you must not underestimate. The very fact that you are a western company setting up in India will give you a status and a quality that you do not have to appreciate in detail, but which you only have to take into account.

If I play up the positives in the next paragraph it is not without experience of the downsides. There are still enough business people in India who have a Nehruvian sense of self sufficiency being the best way forward for them to block out of their consciousness any ideas of the value of liberalised, international trade. There are still resentments and what I have described earlier as a form of inferiority complex that can lead to misunderstandings and worse. I have met Indian business people who, for whatever reason I may like to give, are contemptuous of the West and western business. Without ignoring those threads of feeling, which are important, there is a rich bedrock of positive feeling about the West that I suggest you tap into.

My method below is to bring in some of the negative aspects as I go through the points, but mainly to focus on the positive.

What are the feelings about the West in India today? Of course I am about to generalise and you will find as many views as there are Indians. I am just trying to encapsulate a view.

In discussions with Indian business people, I have tried to sum up that quintessential feeling, and the way of doing that which excites the least contradiction when I am tentatively putting ideas forward is that the West represents an aspiration. A cynical view of the reason why this idea works well is probably that it is fairly vague and can satisfy a number of cases but I think it has more strength than that.

The point is not to forget that India has been for so long a euphemism which is what the phrase *a developing country* has meant. As anyone who has been watching the third and second worlds for any length of time has known, the phrase often meant going backwards rather than any development taking place. Now India is indeed not *a developing country* but a developing country, one that is changing fast and becoming a serious contender on the world economic stage. Indians, no less than other people round the world, have been conscious of this, and now that the first seeds of real development have started to sprout in India, they are beginning to see that a new world is possible for them, for their children and grandchildren.

Aspiration to becoming a developed country underpins much of what India is doing today, and even the association with the other members of the BRICs is really a pragmatic alignment with countries that India sees as developing, and part of a process of moving forward to achieve western standards of living. I would not want anyone to confuse aspirations for that western standard of living with other concepts like western values. You do have to keep those two concepts entirely separate. There are, for example, demographic and social changes in India, such as the fact that there are more marriages for love than ever before but it is from a miniscule base and arranged marriages will remain the norm of the society. Caste will continue to be denied as having any factor within Indian business, but Indian businesses will have a homogeneity of caste within them for the foreseeable future.

Yet the aspiration to be able to live without fear of not having enough food to eat, insufficient water, income that is not dependent upon seasons or the whim of a landlord, is fuelled by an awareness that economic development within India is moving at such a pace that it will be possible for a broader and broader swathe of Indian society to afford western goods. If those two ideas can seem part of the same perspective and not be at odds with each other in your mind, then you are getting somewhere to understanding how the Indian market will be developing and how to approach it.

If you can tap into that sense of aspiration in your marketing, you will be on the way to success. Of course you may well be at some remove from the consumers, but the businesses you may be selling to will be serving that market and working within the same perspective as their customers.

Western goods and services have a number of intrinsic qualities, representing some form of statement about the position of the consumer using them. It is not only that the person who has bought them is successful but far more important than that. They are seen to be thinking ahead, aware of the global market, part of the coming society, and, most importantly, with sufficient aspirations to want to have such products and to be able to show them off.

In marketing terms, this is a potent mixture and one that will reward careful thought.

In practice, balancing this significant thread in consumer consciousness with what can be an equally strong impulse to preserve what is different about being an Indian means that you have a delicate tightrope to walk. This is common in any form of marketing, but it is vital in India. You should be addressing the aspirations of Indians in business or as consumers to become successful as the West is successful, without challenging the values that may be at variance with that aspiration.

If this seems rather pious and rather difficult to grasp, let me focus on one precise example. There are always a number of riots focused on religion in India and there are uneasy relationships between religious groups too. On the other hand there is an engaging — if frustrating — ability to *borrow* another community's religious festivals if there is a public holiday involved. Diwali, also known as Deepavali in south India, is the Hindu festival of lights and the most popular of all the festivals from South Asia. Most commonly Jains and Sikhs will join in, and I have known a good few Muslims and Christians. There is quite an ecumenical feeling in India that God is God however represented.

Diwali is an extensive festival, running over five days, each with a separate significance.

156

The festival celebrates the victory of good over evil, light over darkness, and knowledge over ignorance, but the precise meanings are different in different parts of India. Diwali cards are sent, and greetings exchanged with all sorts of people.

I have known quite a few westerners equate it with Christmas, and there are undoubtedly parallels. The celebrations, with fireworks and lights, and the general enthusiasm the festival creates, are readily recognisable.

But do not step into this area without extreme care and, preferably, trepidation. It sounds obvious enough, but until you understand the extremely difficult vector and nexus between the new world and the old world in India, you will have too many difficulties.

If you have a grasp of motivation and aspiration in India, and how you might play into that area, the second aspect of your go-to-market plan must focus on price. It is often rightly said that price consciousness is at the heart of all Indian psyches, but usually by those who have suffered from it. Like aspiration, pricing is as complex a process in India as in any market which is why the people who can exploit it are well rewarded.

In low end consumer goods and services the actual price, the physical amount, is extremely important. The cola wars in India were fought to pretty much a standstill until one of the combatants introduced a smaller bottle with a lower price — and started cleaning up. You can see how companies such as McDonald's have successfully entered the market in India with tight control over portion size, focused on ensuring that the unit price falls within certain bounds. They have been very successful precisely because of that and it is easy to see how that fits into an aspirational marketing thrust. Although the quantity may be smaller, the consumer is able to demonstrate that he or she is part of the wider world. At the top end of the market, in luxury goods, companies have never cut prices and there is ample evidence of them charging more than they can get away with in the rest of the world. Again it is relatively simple to see how successfully preserving or even enhancing the cachet of such goods exploits the need to demonstrate aspiration.

In the B2B markets, there is obviously a level of indirection, but even here I have known procurement decisions to be taken on the basis of higher prices for western goods. Selling software from the West in India might look very challenging — as indeed it is. Selling it into a state bank where there is sufficient scrutiny of all major deals to discourage any bribery and corruption and where there is a requirement to go for the lowest bidder may look very difficult — as indeed it was and is.

We were not the lowest priced bidder but we won the contract.

We managed this by two interlinked strategies. The first was that we demonstrated that the price we were charging in India was actually significantly less than we charged elsewhere in the world. (You can imagine how hard a balancing trick that was as we had to achieve it without upsetting our pricing structure in the West and yet had to have documented proof. Possible — as we proved — but not for the fainthearted.) At the same time we had to prove that our software offered entirely different qualities for which it was worth paying a premium. (At this point you have to imagine the failure of mental contortions back in head office. The accountants there never quite grasped that selling at 30% below our lowest discount price elsewhere was in fact a premium price in India, and I did have some limited sympathy with their difficulty.)

What we also did was change the relative pricing within the overall package, a fact that caused not only the accountants extreme difficulty but created impossible sums for the heads of the different divisions involved, one of which, in particular, had to accept that the price we were charging for his services in India was not the money he would get in wooden dollars as we had to compensate the other divisional owner for selling at an even lower price. If your internal systems would not be able to cope with such flexibility, you may need to change your systems, or find less drastic solutions.

How this worked in practice was counter intuitive for me. I had produced all sorts of models that reflected my view that western day rates would prove the stumbling block in India. When the cost of labour is so much lower in India this seems to make great sense. We transferred much of the consultancy price into the software pricing. Yet our rather gingerly explorations of this with the client proved the opposite. They could understand that they would have to pay a high rate for western expertise but could not see why they should pay a great deal for what was essentially a sunk cost in the software application.

We also, of course, broke the model down into unit prices, so, in this case, we had a miniscule price for each branch or user of the software. You can understand that that was the headline figure and quite as essential for winning the business.

As you may imagine, the new model eventually presented to the client virtually gave the software away while apparently we had the highest paid consultants in the world working on the project.

In no sense did we try to fool the client and the overall price remained the same, but it was the delicate exploration of each area that eventually gave us the formula we had to use both to appeal to the sensibilities of the bankers involved and to enable us to avoid any sense of using underhand methods.

For me that major balancing act and its subsidiary features were the paradigm that I have encouraged other companies to use when entering the Indian market. It needs to be adapted to your specific market and focus and reviewed on a regular basis because the pricing thresholds are changing so fast, but it still holds good, complete with the encouragement to look surprised in Indian business.

The messages so far are to build on the fact that you are a western company, address the aspirational quality in Indian business and consumer markets, and focus on price looking in two directions at once: low unit pricing and premium pricing where you can or need to. Break any package price down to its units. This does have the danger that you can be negotiated to death over each individual item, but a bit of resolution will get you through that and I will go into that a bit more later.

Beyond those specifics for the Indian market, much of the work that I have completed for clients on their go-to-market strategy has not been superficially much different from working in the West. Inevitably there are subtleties in the Indian experience and it is really important to understand them. They may not make much difference in the long term, but they will probably help you make faster progress.

Differentiation, naturally related to what I have already discussed in this chapter, is as important in India as anywhere. You will find that differentiation is not usually well understood in practice in Indian companies so the subtleties need to be appreciated. If you ask an Indian company how it differentiates its products and services and its approach to the market from its competition, the concept will be readily understood and appreciated. Every Indian company I have met, and every graduate of an Indian Institute of Management for that matter — and there is a good cross over between those two statements — will be prepared to differentiate the company in question from its competition.

The trouble is that nearly all the Indian companies I have dealt with differentiate themselves from their competition not only in the same way but using the same statements. This apparent paradox is difficult to deal with in real life. You will tire of hearing that the company in front of you is different from other Indian companies because not only does it have lower costs, but it has a quality regime second to none, it is extremely responsive to its clients, it works to add value in unexpected ways, and it has extremely low attrition rates. When every company says this — and I am convinced I have seen the same PowerPoint slides from time to time presented by different companies — it is very difficult not to be bored or, and I know this is worse, start to have fun and apparently take the statements seriously.

There is at least one variation creeping into this process because the people in front of you are by no means unintelligent. There is now a suggestion that this differentiation is in fact true despite the fact that every other Indian company differentiates itself in this way because in the current case the suggestion is that other companies are not telling the truth. I think you can guess where this gets to and the epistemological bases of unravelling such statements will either leave you bewildered or you will realise that it is just not worth the effort to understand it fully.

There is, however, a serious clue here for your own differentiation. I know it is full of contradictions, but I also know that you will need to grasp this to be successful. Whatever you finally focus on as your core difference or differences, you will also have to establish something else. You will have to establish that you are in fact very similar to the companies in India that they are already dealing with. Sometimes when I do not manage to explain this very well — I put it down to that — it causes immense confusion. When you are in India, however, differentiating yourself by showing that you are the same as every other competitor will seem quite rational.

It is, of course, a staged process.

I have over time understood the real psychological basis for this. While the Indian company will appreciate the fact that you are a western company and that you therefore have strengths that are different from what is usual, what will be required is the belief that the Indian company can work with you and have confidence in you and the only way to achieve that is by presenting yourself in terms that the Indians can appreciate. In the first place the very fact that you are a western company is probably enough of a differentiator, but just do not stop there. First of all create the awareness that you understand Indian business and that you know how to behave in an Indian context, or at least appreciate that you have to operate differently in an Indian context, and make clear that you will not present too many cultural differences, and at that point start to focus on your differentiators.

Take the key differentiators that the Indians use, especially when dealing with western companies, and see how you can use them for your own benefit.

Quality will be extremely significant — and remember how the perception of what quality is differs between India and the West.

Responsiveness will also be significant and even though you may well regard your company as responsive already you will have to convey this in a different way in India. This is highly sensitive to cultural differences.

If you take the Indian experience of how companies are run as your starting point you will understand both how important responsiveness is and how you have to address it. The key to demonstrating responsiveness to an Indian company usually depends on the quality — not necessarily quantity — of the engagement that the most senior people have with any particular project. In India where the role of middle management is only just emerging in any way and where the hierarchy means that all focus comes from the top of the company, it is wise to suggest how head office at least, and the managing director if possible, will be engaged with the Indian operation. I know that you can demonstrate responsiveness in other ways but unless you can demonstrate how closely the Indian operation is to the heart of the company, you will be battling against a great deal of inbuilt incomprehension. I am not suggesting you make anything up but I am suggesting you maximise any personal involvement.

Demonstrating the added value you can bring is also highly important. One area of expertise that you will have that is of immense value to your Indian clients is your ability to show them how to deal with western companies. You may, as some western clients have suggested to me, feel that this is both obvious and not worth stating. My view is that you take this as extremely important and if you show them how being your customer or client can help them in this regard, you will have achieved a great deal and you will also have reinforced your case for premium pricing — if you need it.

Attrition of skilled personnel is so important in parts of India now that you will need to ensure that your potential Indian clients and customers understand what your level of attrition is and why it is not an issue for you. It may be so little of an issue that you will not even think of it. It will be on your potential clients' mind however, even if, as with every other Indian company, they claim to have extremely low attrition rates, unlike every other Indian company. They key is to extrapolate from your western experience of attrition in order to show how you will address the issues in India.

If you can cover most of these items, you will be on your way to being able to differentiate your business on the basis that it is really not that different from your potential clients' experience.

A focus on benefits and how the features of your product or service will deliver those benefits is just as important in India as it is in the West. The subtlety is that very few Indian companies are yet used to majoring on how managing the benefits into their clients is either possible or desirable. Benefit management may already be second nature to you so that you not only identify the benefits you bring but also how your processes ensure that the benefits are realised in practice. In India this will be quite a novel approach. It will cause some scepticism. It will take extra time and effort both to convey the idea and to show how it will work in practice and give your clients that extra edge in the market place. Nevertheless, I have found it a powerful tool in marketing western companies.

My summary of this part of the go-to-market strategy is therefore: do not forget your normal marketing approach but understand that it will need to respond to the subtleties of the Indian market. Positioning your company and your products and services is still important. Packaging your products and services and developing their benefits — and how you will ensure that the benefits are managed into your clients' businesses — is really important. Performance will be a key as in any part of the world. Persuasion, and how you approach it, is inherent in all that I have described above and I will address it again later in this chapter briefly.

Promotion is the next significant area. The routes to market are varied as they are in any country, and the experience in India will not be that different. I am extremely conscious here of how one size will not fit all — and I have usually worked very hard with individual companies to tailor the public relations and the advertising to their specific needs rather than having a number of simple solutions on tap. We have all the issues of whether you have a requirement for broadcasting or narrowcasting. The fundamental questions, such as will you need to address end users, consumers or trade organisations, still apply.

We rely to some extent on a series of engagements with public relations companies as our major focus is usually B2B businesses. On the other hand, the really important focus in India is on one's personal network, as we have demonstrated throughout this book.

I suppose some sense of what you are up against is the most useful here.

You are intrinsically interesting to the Indian media. I mean by that the very fact that western companies of all shapes and sizes are moving to India in one way or another is still something of a story. There is huge pride that the market in India is now sufficiently compelling for foreign companies to want to enter it. This is coupled with almost the opposite reaction and it even applies to the business correspondents of the national newspapers at times. It is something to be wary of.

The initial business perspective in India that import substitution was the way to success and that the country needed to stand on its own feet to survive and grow, no matter that it has generally been shown to have been more or less unsuccessful, still has a great deal of power. In some circles this would be known as cultural hegemony. If it is unvoiced and generally disregarded that makes this sentiment all the more dangerous, especially if you are unaware of it. In short you are a threat as well as an indication that India is both important and can benefit from what you have to offer.

This will not be surprising in many ways, but the way that it is perceived will be. Borne along by the enthusiasm that you will receive for your engagement with the Indian market from all sorts of Indian business circles and contacts, it is relatively easy to forget that the normal rules of business apply but with an added factor.

You are a competitor and you know that. You are out to take business from other people, and you know that, and the people you engage within the market know that. Both of these are fine.

You are also, however, a representative of another factor: globalisation. Ambivalence about globalisation is not restricted to the West. I do not have to go very deeply into this for you to realise that this can be a potent counter to the immediate interest you will generate. I have known a number of companies taken unawares by this so it is not always perceived, no matter that in the cold light of day it might seem obvious.

You therefore have a very fine line to walk when dealing with Indian media. I have seen companies take on a very humble approach which is superficially sensible but not very satisfactory either in the short or long term. If you can somehow present your company as wanting to work with India and learn from India, if you can stress how significant the Indian contribution to science and learning has been, and if you can admire the growth of Indian companies, you can make a certain amount of headway.

The problem is that you might win the battle but you will lose the war.

None of these sentiments is bad in itself, and I commend them to you for the appropriate time and place — and there will be an appropriate time and place for all of them. Do be conscious that they undermine what you are really doing, and I am a great believer that all marketing has to be fact based and consistent with your long term goals. After all, you want to make money out of India and you will be doing so by exploiting gaps in the market, squeezing out the competition, and possibly creating unemployment before you make any real contribution to employment.

The answer that has been successful in all my dealings with India has focused on the benefits that you are bringing to India. As a salesman

I suppose I could do no other but this is the story that will have the fewest comebacks. I have been known to explain how there are immediate issues with what we are doing once I have stressed the benefits.

My approach is best summed up in this sentence: *We do understand that there are growing pains but the immediate and future benefits are the most important element that we are bringing to this market.*

This is also the story that will attract most media interest. So the question I always ask our clients is what benefit will it be to India if you enter that market? If they are clear what that is, then media questioning, engagement with interest groups, discussions with bureaucrats and politicians and interaction with trade bodies and other organisations will be straightforward without sacrificing the truth that you are out to make money.

With that warning in mind, let us still understand the excitement that there will be in you entering the local market in India, whether that is in a metro or in a smaller region. The usual western warnings about making sure that you have a co-ordinated launch, that you keep your powder dry until you are established and ready to roll, that you ensure that there is a rolling programme of information dissemination after the launch, and that you do not neglect the public relations opportunities you will have, all apply.

The advantage you have is that you will be interesting. You will be expected to have opinions. You will, of course, receive set backs in the media. Yet you are a story — and every public relations executive will tell you how important that little fact is. You do not have to create interest — you have to ensure you address it in the right way.

And if you need broadcasting for your message to the market, do not forget the new multiplex cinemas in India. These are probably, in the way that television is not, the most universal experience that your end consumers have. Television in India has gone from being quite homogenous to a splintered, extraordinarily diverse market within less than five years. It is ideal if you want to address a narrow niche, murder if you want some mass appeal. Do not forget the web, either. The Internet is as universal as in the West — and even more powerful amongst its users, who rely on it in a way that perhaps only those under 20 in the West rely on it.

Selling in India is relentless in a way that you would not have experienced before. It is not only the bombardment of advertising that I mean, but the single minded insistence behind it. As we have seen, negotiation in India is almost purely a statement and re-statement of the same points until one of you buys or dies. Selling is almost the same. In India, you only need repetition, it seems to me, to be successful — or, rather, without repetition you cannot be successful.

One example of a failure to sell to me might show you much more than any examples of successful selling.

I was being sold the benefits of working with a particular company. I was battered and battered by the person selling — an engaging character who would occasionally pause for breath and who was obviously from the purest form of Indian sales practice, the one which seems to believe that listening is all very well in its place. His presupposition was that I would buy. Not only that, but for me not to buy was going to affect my future in some serious but unspecified ways. He had no doubts about my need to buy into the vision he had, my propensity to buy and the general efficacy of the whole process. In terms of belief he was the sort of person that you would dread to turn up on your doorstep in the West and persuade you to their way of religion.

Crucially, he was obviously successful in his way of progressing his own business and approach in India.

Having given all the possible non-buying signals that I could muster, from gentle hints at the beginning such as *I am not at all interested in working with you*, through to looking at the spreadsheet in front of me on my laptop that bore no relation to what he was talking about, I was still further battered and bruised for a couple of hours. At the end of it all he remained unconvinced that I was in any way serious about not wanting to work with him, but he shook my hand and we talked, inevitably, about cricket. I was bewildered but he was not in the least fazed by any of it. For me it had been a traumatic interruption of life as I knew it and a waste of very good time. To him it had been just another sales encounter.

Persistence and repetition are the hallmarks of Indian selling and then, in turn, the negotiation process. You will need to be aware of how persistent you need to be because western standards will not equip you for the siege mentality you will need to adopt in India.

To sell well in India you need assertiveness of the kind that looks like aggression. You will need it in buckets — and that is why the people you appoint to work for you and with you in India are so important. It is also why appointing such people is so crucial — and, often, so difficult.

TEN

STAFFING IN INDIA AND GLOBAL TALENT MANAGEMENT

Before we go any further we have to focus on staffing in India. The key issue at this point addressing anywhere in the world would be your staff, and it is so important, I am devoting a whole chapter to it. More than just setting up in another western country, which can be traumatic enough, setting up in India will tax you hard in terms of the people you will employ. It will tax your human resources people. It will tax your existing staff in your home country. This is a vital consideration that is sometimes forgotten. There will inevitably be a focus on communication whenever you deal with India, not least in this book, but do remember the importance of communicating with your current staff, early and often.

If you think this is too obvious to state, I can only tell you that I have seen enough examples where that was largely forgotten until a crisis was caused.

It is easily done. The concerns, and often the excitement, of setting up in India can quite easily take your mind off what is closest to you, and I have found creating a communication plan focused on your existing staff well in advance is time well spent.

One reason is that India represents so many different ideas in western business consciousness. The most potent perspective is the one that says that a job — and usually that becomes *my job* — may well be outsourced to India. Creating your business venture in India may be entirely different in your mind, but it can trigger a whole series of almost autonomic reactions.

I have seen it more than once.

You will know when it is the right time to announce your plans to go into the Indian market. Timing as with so many things in business is the point to focus on. It is highly important that you are prepared and have taken into account the worst imaginings of your current staff.

In India itself you will have a different focus. The person specification that you arrive at for your main manager at least will be dependent upon how you intend to go to market and that is why this chapter follows that discussion.

To understand what your specification and the job description that you create from it will contain, you have to understand a great deal about your own company and the way to go forward in India. If that seems a strange order — your company first, then India — it is nevertheless undoubtedly right.

It is also important to be aware of another aspect of going to India, and that is the quality of people that you will be dealing with and the way that this might make a difference to your company in the rest of the world. I mentioned this as a hidden benefit, and I do suggest that you bring this out as you develop the Indian operation. It is an enormous plus.

As I said above, there are some key elements in your own company that will influence your approach to recruitment in India. The first to grapple with and one that generally causes quite a lot of head scratching is whether you will export a manager, probably temporarily, or whether you will start with an Indian manager. The latter is the brave way and one that may also be seen as foolhardy although I have seen it done successfully. Despite all the issues that an expatriate can bring, I tend to go that way. It really does depend on whether your company is capable of absorbing a new culture, allowing your Indian company to have its own distinctive culture, or whether you are really conscious of your corporate culture and believe that it must run through all parts of the company.

Whichever it is, it will involve quite a degree of training, either in the West or in India. No matter how strong the training is, if you appoint an Indian from the start you will find that your Indian company will obviously be much more Indian than western. It is a matter of degree of course as whatever you do, there will be distinctive elements of India in your Indian subsidiary. It is a question of primacy and emphasis.

The second element in your own company that will influence the appointment of an expatriate or an Indian will come down to how independence is viewed. For some companies the balance sheet is all — and as long as the subsidiary operates within the budgets that have been agreed, how it operates on a day to day basis is of little importance. For others, it is essential to have a tight knit overall operation and conformity to standard operating procedures, modified to some extent of course. In that case there is no option but to export your own manager.

The third element is reporting methods and here the difference between having a westerner and having an Indian can be significant. There is a quality in Indian reporting which is best described as back to one of my key phrases for India: *that'll do*. If your head office can deal with that and take it in its stride, you will not have the same difficulties as others have starting with an Indian as the head of your company.

I am not suggesting that you will necessarily have great difficulties, or any fraud or real problems, but if you think how you might have approached being a general manager approving accounts going to head office in the West, you will know that you will have taken certain decisions about how the figures were presented. You might have smoothed certain elements of sales or expenditure, for example. I certainly did. Head office will have shared some of the same basic assumptions and been able to second guess what was happening. You will not quite know when you get figures from India from an Indian manager what lies behind them — and yet you will know that something has happened to the raw figures. If that is coupled with a different sense of time and date so that what is only expected to be, might actually have taken on reality in the figures — as can happen in India — you will be rather at sea.

My bias is obvious in all this and I think the best way forward is to have your own western person on the spot to start with. He or she will take a great deal of training — much of it informal, just watching and listening — and will not be anywhere near as effective as an Indian in getting the place started and making it function, but it will have the major advantage that you will have your own ears and eyes and you will understand.

When I say that there will be an enormous training requirement for a westerner going to India to manage for the first time, this would be mirrored by having an Indian in place learning to work within your organisation. To be more specific about some of the areas, think of these:

- How you approach relationships
- How you establish trust
- Punctuality and time keeping
- Ensuring legal commitments are kept
- Management style
- Teamwork style
- Interpersonal styles
- Meeting styles
- Initiative and following instructions
- Attitudes to mistakes
- Approach to processes and procedures
- Conflict resolution
- The business implications of a different culture

Each of these areas will need a specific focus for a westerner to be able to deal with them.

To take but one example, there will be some incomprehension about a westerner's approach to setting up appointments with potential clients or customers. Whereas you might think giving someone notice of an appointment is entirely reasonable, in an Indian context it will apparently be accepted but have little validity. The Indian concept of business is so fast moving that the idea of giving anyone more than a few days notice of wanting to see them will be regarded as at best quaint. If you want to see someone, then it is perfectly obvious you need to see them now.

If not — do you really need to see them?

This perspective caused me all sorts of grief when I was first trying to do business in India, as opposed to dealing with Indians in the west. It is actually quite a corrective to the western view of executive time — it might not be right in a western context, but it does have merit and made me change some of my approach back in the West — both as a person potential suppliers wanted to see and as a person who wanted to see senior managers in a company I wanted to work with.

To an Indian business person, the idea of today is perfectly reasonable. Tomorrow has a real quality about it and a sense of commitment. In my experience going beyond that you reach the limits of what an Indian business person considers worth holding in his or her head. They will say yes without any sense that this is a commitment as it is too far away to matter.

To take another, the attitude of a western manager to mistakes and getting things wrong by his or her staff is absolutely crucial and one where I made my biggest mistake when I was first managing director. And this despite the fact that — I am conscious that I have made as many mistakes as anybody else. I am not that certain that I have spotted all that I have made, though over the years I have had my fair share pointed out to me. Helping someone who has made a mistake learn from it is enshrined in all sorts of management advice and in the West it is just about possible to go through the process of identifying someone's mistake and help them profit from it. I say that it is just about possible, because any manager will know how tricky it is to do so and still have the person you are talking to realise that he or she is valued.

In India the hierarchical nature of business society is such that before you establish any of your other concepts of management in India, the slightest attempt to deal with a mistake or a wrong decision can be perceived as bullying. There will be a real sense of humiliation, even if the discussion takes place in private and is completely apparently supportive — as well as justified. If after nearly eight years I sound wary, you can see the effect one particular incident had on me.

As far as I was concerned a number of fairly low level decisions about time allocation had been taken wrongly by a salesman. After about a month, I thought I knew him well enough — and, more importantly, he knew me well enough — to take him through the issues and establish better practice. I conducted the meeting like many I had in the West. The result was an apparently stoical person opposite me. After the meeting, one of his colleagues came to see me to tell me that I had really destroyed him. In turn I was immediately devastated. I tried to make amends, I apologised both for the way I had conducted the meeting and the fact that I had not understood, and over time we established a good working relationship.

What I had done in his terms was to use my position in a way that meant that he could not answer me back and, more importantly, could not make any attempt to justify his decisions. In western terms I was hardly assertive. In Indian terms I had unfairly attacked him. I am pleased to say that later he was one of the delegation who came to tell me that I had got so much wrong that in future I was not the managing director, but the *managed* director. This, in Indian terms, was almost unthinkable and I took it as a compliment. In fact, after that he did properly get to know and understand me, and, I do not know if I am delighted to say, he treated me with the respect I deserved. But that level of sensitivity has remained with me.

Redirecting someone — let alone telling them off — is extraordinarily difficult across cultures, and you might like to reflect that when you can do that effectively you have reached quite a level of understanding. Until that happens, you will have to tread carefully and probably do what I did, which is to do it indirectly, through another Indian. You can imagine how difficult it is to select the right person to bear this burden, but that is another story.

This points to another element of Indian business life which is related to management style. Obviously you will have as many styles as there are managers, but it is knowing where in the international spectrum of formality versus informality India sits that is crucial.

When I am dealing with this I draw the spectrum between two areas I have worked in: Germany and the US. To an outsider German business is conducted with a formality that is daunting, with the correct title given to every individual — and in Germany it can be titles as one is added to the other rather than one replacing the former. I think the expression I witnessed of *herr professor doctor* is probably an exception even for Germany, but even so, used between two people who had shared the same office for five years, it was thought provoking. (I never discovered whether in the privacy of their own company they managed to drop any or all of the titles.) Against the German experience there is the American experience of easy adoption of first names and a sense of being old buddies with someone even before you have exchanged details of any surgical operations you have had, which sometimes seem to me to be the staple of such conversations, but that is probably down to age.

In India you can use first names — well, the name that is used by their friends and relatives which might not be the first name — in just the same way as the US. Do not take this, however, as a sign that informality is acceptable in the office.

If I take the UK experience, different again from the US, India and Germany, you might see more clearly what I mean. It is only because of my experience with other business cultures that I have been able to tease out the British approach and its peculiarities. In discussions with a Brit you will in general meet a whole series of guarded statements. These are like fences. To another Brit these are markers of where subsequent conversations may go and any Brit will make a, probably subconscious, note of the areas. If you get a *not really* response from a Brit, you will know what I mean. It does not signify a lack of substance in anything, only that it is too early to discuss such a matter. At a later date you will be able to address this particular item which is not really anything at the first meeting and find out what it means. You just will not get any further at the point when it is first said. In short you have to peel back the onion over time.

In the US my experience is that what can be discussed comes out pretty quickly and there are not quite these same markers. What is private to an American will not be signalled but will just not come out in any business relationship unless that relationship moves to a much deeper, probably social, level. You will get a great deal more at first and then apparently less.

In India it is a mixture of the two plus a Germanic reserve. In short over a great deal of time I have managed to discuss caste, arranged marriages, and the way that religion writhes through Indian society with my business asso-ciates, but later reference to them even between two people on their own is outside the scope of a business relationship.

The message is to be relaxed in the office, but maintain a distance that is quite apparent. I draw attention to it as it will really need attention from any western manager.

The overall result is that having a western manager is not going to be the easiest way forward even with the most culturally attuned individual, but I have come to the conclusion that it is the most effective. After all, it has to be a process of acclimatisation or, as some would have it, acculturalisation. It is my estimation that you will want to ensure that a very real sense of your values and approach permeates the fabric of the organisation and allow that to sit alongside the special qualities that an Indian company should have.

One of the first priorities that a western manager should have is the iden-tification of his or her successor as succession planning is really important. It should not be a fast process, but if you have a western manager in place ensure that the search is on as soon as possible for the Indian successor. You will be recruiting a manager so do make sure that you recruit someone who has the potential for the overall role.

I know that here there are at least two perspectives on finding the right people for your company in India. We have been asked to take both routes, but our experience suggests one as the more successful route. It comes down to experience. Our view is that you should recruit someone with the barest minimum of experience but the greatest aptitude. If that seems obvious in so many ways, especially in the light of the rest of the book, I do have to show you why the alternative approach is often favoured.

The argument we encounter takes many forms, but it generally comes down to this: *India is such a challenge anyway, we need to be able to take for granted experience in our business domain as well as skills in our product sets so we can inculcate and ourselves absorb the different business environment.* It is not a meretricious argument at all, much as you would expect, because it is used by intelligent and experienced business people. The trouble for us is that it implies a great deal of unlearning. Someone recruited with domain experi-ence and the full set of managerial tools and skills will have to unlearn many of them. I have discovered over the years that if I find learning something difficult, unlearning something that I have come to rely on is a quantum leap in difficulty.

I think competency-based interviewing and the other techniques you might use in the West are fine in their way, but what I am looking for now in the senior manager for a new company in India is aptitude, flexibility and an interest in people. I would rather train than untrain someone.

Whether you are going to have a western senior manager and want to employ an Indian number two or start with an Indian, your first difficulty will be identifying potential candidates, and this will be for two reasons. The first is that you will be overwhelmed if you advertise. If you do not advertise, you will not know where to start. Executive search companies do exist now in India, and they are starting to be effective, but in general, the route has to be the channel we identified chapters ago: the brother-in-law or the cousin — in short the network.

Advertisements are very much a two edged sword. It is nothing to receive five or six thousand responses to an advertisement for a role. In general you will be able to whittle them down successfully to 50 to 100 without much trouble but only by taking a great deal of time. It may well be worth it and for companies set up to deal with this scale of response it is relatively straightforward. I have to say on the other hand that it is whittling on a grand scale. We do, when pushed, adopt this method and have used it successfully.

We prefer to use the network. People understand the concept behind six degrees of separation — that is you can probably get to anyone in the planet through six people, of whom you know well enough the first two. In India, it is the way to start recruitment. The only reassurance I need to give at this point is that just like in the West, you will know when you have the right person for you. We have used all sorts of psychometric tests, and all sorts of recruitment tests, but we have generally known when the right person is in front of us. We then take up references in some detail. No matter how reliable the cousin or brother-in-law might appear, do so. As in the West, the value of the reference is as much in the selection of the referee as in the statements that the referee will give. If the referee is unlikely to be closely related to the potential employee, sufficiently senior to take an objective view and to have a reputation to defend, the reference is likely to have more value, even if it is more negative than you might expect or want.

Having recruited the right person, think about retention. It is true that India has a surplus of labour, and the surplus is somewhere in every level of business, but once you have found someone, we think it is far too damaging to lose them, even to be replaced with what on paper might be a better person. If you think of the scale of training we have suggested, you will understand what we mean.

There is another real benefit to working on retention at this point. If you have any concerns at all about lacking the right degree of talent in your organisation, and most that we talk to in the West are aware of the fight for talent in their industries, managing the talent that you come across in India is even more important than it might be for its immediate benefit in India. If you think of the different qualities that India is bringing to business life, especially in terms of flexibility and adroitness in developing new ways of doing business, any Indians you recruit into senior positions will have a value for your talent pool within the company. They may never leave India, but they will still be able to add value to your company, if you take steps to enable them to do so.

In fact that is the first step to retention in India. Of course all the normal steps to retention apply, like providing effective training and career development opportunities, appropriate remuneration and stretching intellectual challenges, but the most important for you is the fact that you are a western company. To be part of such a company is important in India, no matter that you are small or even insignificant.

Being part of a company, however, does not rely on being *a* or even *the* senior manager in India, it is being recognised as an important contributor to the company as a whole that is the first step to retention. If this seems too obvious, plenty of companies seem to forget it — and attrition amongst senior members of staff, especially those trained by western companies, is always high. By all means use sticks to keep people, like freezing bonuses until a period of time has passed by especially if you can be substantially into the next bonus period before you pay them out, but in India, as in most places, it is the carrots that are successful.

How bonuses are established by companies is probably less important than the fact that they are. The areas that we have found most successful, however, are focused in India on the goals for your company as a whole, as well as those based eventually on individual performance. We think it is essential to have shared goals across the company and to make India part of the company from day one. It follows that India has to have a direct understanding and interest in the overall goals of the company.

Building shared goals, which obviously contributes to the focus above, but is actually a different perspective, is the next step. When you are reasonably established in India, build or rebuild your corporate goals together with your Indian team, starting, if not from scratch, at least from pretty well the basics that you understand about your business. It does take time, but it does mean that retention is easier, and, also, the spirit in the company improves because, however tedious it might seem to go over familiar ground, you will learn something new and engage with different brains.

Our experience is then to take this down below the Indian management level, and engage, initially at least, on team based goals, rather than individual objectives. You will have objectives for each person, but it is vital to ensure that the objectives you set contribute to, and if possible are subsets of, the team goals, as you will want to engender a real sense of belonging to the organisation.

Then be aware of the special effects in India of the idea that knowledge is power. It is a question here of publicly acknowledging the special understanding that your Indians will bring to your corporate life. In effect, power should be possible in many places.

And retention in India depends, as it does elsewhere, on communication. It can be as simple as having video conferences. This may conjure up in your mind special rooms with expensive equipment. For one company that was deeply sceptical about how effective a very simple arrangement could be, I ensured that we had an inexpensive camera linked to a notebook computer at each end, and then had regular updates. When we reached the point where it was no novelty to see the Indians in India, and to see the western management team in the West, we started to have an exchange of views, an immediate lift in spirits and a greater determination to do well. Both sides identified with the other in a way that was difficult to imagine without this simple expedient.

My final element in the retention of the most senior member of your Indian office does take time, and effort, and commitment — and trust. In fact, it will occur at the moment when trust is established. When I am setting up such an arrangement, I make it clear what a milestone it will be and how it will mark the coming of age of the subsidiary. It is the moment when you move from managing to monitoring your Indian operation. It could well be the moment when your western manager leaves that office or it could be when you tell your Indian manager that the Indian subsidiary has come into its own, but it is the single most important moment in the developing maturity of your operation offshore. It is no different from anywhere else in the world, apart from the sensitivities of the Indians involved. It will be extra special to them — and to you.

By setting this as one of your most important goals — and often I make it the most important — you will achieve an enormous amount when you reach this milestone.

There are subsidiary elements to achieving this aim. For example, you will need to create a performance management regime from the start, and you will need to work very hard with your Indian counterparts to ensure that all sides understand that trust is not only earned but is reinforced by every action. Moving to monitoring will be the most important recognition of this milestone.

I have rather fudged remuneration, by the suggestion that it is at an appropriate level. I have covered some of the issues in earlier chapters, but remember purchasing power parity and different standards of what is considered civilised life in different parts of the world, and you will have the right yardsticks.

The benefits of establishing yourself in India will not only be the additional revenues and profit you will generate, and nor just the way that a different perspective will be brought to your business. For many companies there is an absolute gain and benefit out of the extremely daunting task of knowledge transfer.

In order to function at all in India you will need to capture what you know about business in the West. I have known companies that found this irksome to an extreme. One client even said to me that had they known the pain this particular element would cause them — and the costs associated with it — they were not sure they would have embarked on such a pro-gramme. I say this so you will take it seriously as a non-trivial task.

If one of the most important lessons from business for you is that you should always reduce what you do to the simplest elements and then wrap it up in a process so that the lowest possible level of employee can do the task, then this will not be a surprise. Many companies, however, know this in an intuitive sort of way, but never quite get round to implementing it.

Please note that I did not mean that you should only employ the lowest skilled people. I have been misunderstood like that, and it is easy to do. The message is that you should always use the lowest level of skill that can do the task, and if that happens to be a PhD in rocket science, then so be it, but if by trapping and transferring the knowledge and skills involved in a process, you can give it to a lowly soul who only has a masters in rocket science, then so much the better.

Opening in India will give you a firm incentive to capture all your processes, skills and knowledge so they can be carried out in India — and modified in due course by the Indians. You can then examine very carefully who you need in India, and then analyse in detail whether the skill levels you employ in the West are still appropriate, or whether you can use your highly trained and expensive western staff in more productive ways. One company we worked with had this idea from the start and although they found the pain of creating processes and procedures as difficult as any other company, the benefits they achieved are still standing them in good stead now.

From the start in India, take this a little further and create your own data-base of the lessons you learn. I know one company that captured them in a spreadsheet which was highly organised of them and probably effective. The most inventive way, and the company that got the best out of it, captured it as a presentation which it added to and changed on a relatively frequent basis. The point was that from the start the lessons were to be shared.

The most important idea to bear in mind about India and staffing is that it will be as frustrating and as tedious and endless as it is in the West. To go with any other perspective will be to mislead yourself. Staffing is self-evidently about people and people are both rewarding and frustrating and usually not in equal measure. India will not be any different.

Keep in mind the fact that most management is communication and that you have to have a communications plan to be successful in India as elsewhere. The only difference is that you should use the communications plan as a check list to ensure that you are dealing with all the people you have to address.

In any case, you can guarantee that at least half of your communications will either be misunderstood or, worse, misinterpreted. If you can imagine the potential for chaos in such a statement, you are probably well on your way to being able to take a senior position in India or advise someone else how to.

As time passes, and as India becomes more like the West in business terms, you may want to think that this will make it easier. In my experience it becomes easier to make mistakes. In my time of dealing with India I have seen massive changes and India has become apparently less strange and less daunting. Paradoxically I see this as a bigger trap. If you think India looks like something you know, you are not really dealing with the real level you must grapple with. If it seems strange and daunting, it is and you are perceiving the right degree of difficulty.

ELEVEN

TURNING THESE INSIGHTS INTO REAL BUSINESS ADVANTAGE

It is now that the adventure can really begin. Of course, you will have gone to India before you have reached this position in reality because, as I have written many times, there is just no substitute for seeing India and Indian business at first hand. Now with all the planning to support you, and the various insights that you have gleaned from all sorts of sources as well as this book, you are poised to take the big step.

Having got to the position where you understand the opportunity, have examined your business in detail and created a business case and a business plan for entering the Indian market, got some sort of implementation plan and a way of recruiting your staff, you are close to starting the actual process of entering the Indian market. There will still, however, be huge gaps in understanding and details of what you can do. This book cannot hope to fill in the missing links entirely, but can point you in the right directions.

As with any country, there are a mass of statistics and insights available on the web. I do not, as I have written earlier, trust any of them. I trust the trends that are revealed but the naked figures mean as much or as little as the person or organisation who commissioned them. It is probably ingenuous of me to say that I was initially shocked at the way that international consultancies could be prevailed upon to endorse any figures that their sponsors might like them to validate. Nevertheless I would not trust the figures given by such organisations any more than I would trust the statistics emanating from Indian organisations. There is just too much at stake — both ways.

You will need to garner information about India and the market as it develops. We usually do some relatively high level market research for our clients prior to starting serious work with them, and we use a variety of resources. You will find no paucity of information — in many cases just the reverse.

The Web is obviously a good place to start and over the years I have had great enjoyment reading Web sites dedicated to Indian industry. You might think that a strange way of having fun — and it is — but for a student of English in all its varied forms, it can be a real pleasure.

The Associated Chambers of Commerce and Industry of India, for example, starts off its history:

> Chronicling evolution of the chamber posits the advantage of stating at the outset, the schematic unfolding of the tapestry of events that eventually concluded in contrasting interests federating into a coalition of mercantile consolidation.[1]

I am not sure what it means, but you cannot deny it is stately and imposing and has a great conviction in its own value. ASSOCHAM, as it calls itself, does have some useful information as well, of course.

The Confederation of Indian Industry is obviously very useful too, particularly with its focus on areas such as logistics. It, like many Indian sites, has a series of newsletters that it issues and I have found them of value mainly as email alerts to new developments. It is particularly useful for some of my clients because it has a focus on the small and medium enterprise (SME)

---

[1] http://www.assocham.org/about/history.php.

and being in touch with the CII, as it is known, has real advantages. It can, for example, be your first introduction to a network of people in India.

I often turn to the Indian Brand Equity Foundation or IBEF for up to date information and insights. The foundation does provide a full range of insights and does cover each industry group, from agriculture to media, from power to business process outsourcing, and it also has a newsletter that is sometimes rather over the top in its trumpeting of Indian achievements, but once you discount that, it does provide a range of insights into not only what is happening but what influential people in India regard as important enough to draw attention to.

There are various trade journals and business directories, such as, jimtrade. com, and these are as useful or as useless as they are in any country. I have not been a great fan of them over the years except as general indications of the state of the market. If you enter a product category and not much appears it does tell you something about the market and the value of entering it. It is not, of course, fool proof either way. If there is no mention of a particular product it might be really good news for you. On the other hand I always like to know that there is competition around so I am not faced with creating an audience and a market from scratch.

Each of the Indian embassies and their equivalent in the UK, the Indian High Commission, provide newsletters and create events. I subscribe to some. As you may be aware from reading this book, I am not the greatest fan of the Indian diplomatic staff in terms of actually promoting trade between India and the West. I have met some of the most absolutely engaging and capable individuals working in them, but I have come to the conclusion that the terms of reference that they work to are not in line with what I would expect. I am sure that my experience cannot be that representative and it is relatively easy to arrange an appointment and understand what they have to offer.

On the other hand, what I have found useful are the various trade missions that arrive from individual states, shepherded by the embassy or high commission. For that reason, if for no other, I do recommend that you keep in touch with the trade and industry section of your local embassy or high commission. The various incentives that individual states offer in particular market sectors are sufficiently interesting to be worth understanding. The usual caveats apply, such as checking that what is described as an incentive that only this particular state offers is in fact that exclusive. The competition between the states in sufficient to merit keeping a good eye on what is going on in each of them. As one example the state of Maharashtra, where Mumbai is located, has a Web site where economic statistics are maintained and, perhaps more importantly, tenders are published. You may not wish to submit a proposal in response, but they do give good insights into what is happening at a state level. The government of Tamil Nadu, as another example, has an interesting document about its industrial policy and it contains this statement:

The following are the key objectives of the Industrial Policy:

- To position Tamil Nadu as the most attractive investment destination
- To facilitate industry capturing a larger share of world trade in goods/ services
- To reform regulatory processes and remove procedural hurdles in business
- To enable integration of existing industrial clusters with global supply chains
- To build efficient and dependable industrial infrastructure
- To develop human resources and intellectual capital to world standards
- To encourage symbiosis with SMEs in major industry clusters

Again the focus on SMEs has proved very interesting to some of our clients, while there is also a clear warning in the third item about the hidden barriers to entry!

This book is not a catalogue of Web sites — but there is an appendix of some of the more useful ones — and most people engaged in market research will be able to find a mass of information that will prove useful.

There is no substitute, however, for going once you have created the plan for your business. I know this may sound obvious but somehow forming the best possible plan does sometimes dominate thinking. Getting there and discussing your plans — as vaguely as possible, I suggest, in order to protect yourself and your plans — is crucial.

It is also crucial to prepare yourself for how your plans will be analysed and commented upon. They will almost without exception be excellent plans. They will have just the right balance between risk and certainty. You will receive a whole hearted and undoubted *yes*. If you ask for an opinion, you will get the closest that the people listening to you can approximate to what they think you would expect.

Do not trust a word of it.

There is a method of getting round it, but it has a little flaw that you have to work round. The approach I use to circumvent the innate politeness — for that is what drives the positive response — is to suggest that you have been granted access to some business plans by another organisation. These plans seem to you to be wrong headed and really not to understand much about the Indian market. If you then ask for some analysis and commentary on them you will not be out of the woods yet. Naturally you will get the answer they expect you want. It is the same danger with an opposite effect.

What I have found, however, is that it is a good deal easier to tease out the strengths and weaknesses as properly perceived by Indian business people coming from this angle.

The way that I get under the radar is to let my opposite number tell me how poor the plan is in some detail. There will be valuable insights in this, but it will not be worth much as a coherent analysis. I then start to suggest that there are valuable elements. I suppose it is a form of torture watching someone who is too polite to contradict me attempting to face in two directions at once, but it does work as a method of finding out the real view of the business plan. The only way I salve my conscience is that I always tell my victim — my business associate, I mean — what I have done and, most importantly, why I have done it. I do that afterwards, of course. I have always had a good humoured acceptance — at least to my face — and a recognition that in order to get the truth this is the sort of subterfuge that is required.

If this seems a rather involved process, let me assure you of the value. Of course it does depend upon the capability of the Indian business person you are talking to, but I have never yet failed to gather some useful insights and some incisive criticisms and pointers from such discussions. It is the difference between a native speaker of a language and a person who speaks the language as a second language. All the intonation and accent and pronunciation will be there, but there will be just that lack of local knowledge. Always trust the native speaker.

I guess that what I am really saying is go and kick a few tyres. What that really means is something different. Try and buy what you are hoping to sell. My advice is to do this as often as you can. Watch how the sales process is initiated, taken through its natural cycle and then moved to a close. Our biggest focus as a consultancy is usually on whether there is any sales process or whether it is order taking — but you will know best for your own particular industry.

If there is no chance of buying what you are hoping to sell, it is, as we have discussed earlier, a double edged sword. There will be no competition. There will also be no ready audience and market. That is useful information in its own right. Do, however, persevere as there will be analogous products and services which will give you at least some indication and talking to sales people is usually not a waste of time in market research. You may even identify someone you would like to employ.

Obviously you can conduct the research into sales people from your home country — but I take it that you will be there at various stages to test your approach and your theories and I have to say that you really have to be in India to appreciate the differences and to be able to understand.

I am very conscious of the differences I see between Indian sales people and what would be the general common standard in the West. It is impossible to generalise, but I think it is as well to understand some of the characteristics. The key word that I would keep in mind is *relentless*. In some western sales environments this is more highly prized than in others, but overall you will find that there is a quantum difference between your understanding of relentless, even if the concept is formed by the picture of a double glazing sales person in Texas, and how Indian sales people are.

I am not making a qualitative statement here — it is not that one is better than the other. It is just how relentless an Indian can be. Imagine that the sales training given to such people is focused on one and only one adage: *you would not have had this opportunity to sell without there being a bit of interest in what you have to sell. It is your job as a sales person to turn that little bit of interest into the undoubted sale that this implies.*

Be prepared to be wrestled to the ground by the sales people you phone.

The process of phoning some existing sales people is one of the first steps to understanding how you can measure success in India. You will naturally have your revenue targets, your milestone of when you will become cash positive and then the point where you break even and, from there, start being profitable. All of those measures are important. Nevertheless in a new country it is advisable to have other benchmarks — softer ones, probably, as well — which will give you other indications of progress.

Track enquiries of course. Monitor your sales people as you would do normally, but monitor them against the enquiries you made when you were doing the work above and watch how they handle enquiries. Having talked to Indian sales people as a customer you will be better able to judge the sales person's capability — but more importantly, judge his or her mood, attitude and approach. In your first months that will be a good guide to how successful you are being.

As a salesman myself, I always think that sales people are the best litmus paper for an enterprise. I think the collective noun of sales people is *a whinge*. If they are not making some noise — and complaining — they are not doing enough. If they are making too much noise — you have to do something about it, as there is something serious that is preventing them from focusing on moaning about the customers. If they are making no noise at all you are either paying them too much or not stretching them, or, as the finance director usually believes, they are actually dead. That is why watching your sales people in India and listening to the general level of noise and whingeing is so important for a soft measure of how well you are doing. The added indicator for India is how aggressive they appear to you to be. If they seem acceptably aggressive — worry as they are not performing well. They should be off your scale.

As in indication of how strange this has to be to show you that they are performing, I am still surprised when I hear an Indian sales person discussing a deal with a western company in the West. In context — in India — I have got my understanding at the right pitch. When I am in the West it comes across as strange. Indeed when we do sales training for Indian companies in the West almost the main focus is changing their understanding of what is assertive and what is aggressive.

On the other hand, I have had immense difficulty trying to reproduce that aggression myself when I am in India dealing with an Indian client. No matter that I have listened and watched and tried to learn, my form of strengthened forcefulness is just wrong for India. It is just not understood. I think I am mimicking what I see and hear but it is perceived differently. There is a part of me that suggests that again this is context. Indians are not used to a westerner behaving like this and therefore it just does not compute.

The answer is to be firm and let your Indian sales people take the lead.

One area, however, where you can intervene and improve almost any Indian sales person's performance is by stressing the importance of listening. All sales people pay lip service to listening. I am sure it was a sales person who invented *active listening* — which turns out in most cases to be talking. I used to give my sales people targets in terms of understanding the customers and clients. We used to hold our sales meetings at the beginning of the week so we did not look back and we could adequately plan for tomorrow, but in that meeting I would ask what new fact or ideas each of them had picked up from the client the previous week. This produced a different mind set and after a while I was rewarded with little nuggets. The facts were not important, but changing the approach to listening was.

The overall message is that, as with all measurements in India, western scales are not the most reliable indicator.

The most difficult aspect of measuring success in India is related to the different scale and is really a product of the success that you can have. It is understanding how successful you are relative to the opportunity there is. If your market sector is growing at 20% in India and you are growing at less than that after establishing your company, you are obviously not doing well. This is perfectly clear. Nevertheless, I have had clients who have not taken into account the relative rate of growth and really been pleased with what they are achieving. For those of us in the West used to single digit growth rates it is quite easy to fall into this trap and I have seen very experienced business development managers and directors fail to recalibrate their expectations.

In my experience there is not an antidote to this lack of common scales and calibration except being in India — and even then it is very hard. The only way that I have been successful is by remaining aware of the issue all the time.

My analogy is driving position. In India, like in the UK, cars are meant to drive on the correct side of the road. In almost the rest of the world they drive on the right side. That is, in India, they drive on the left. (In general this is true, but it is not something you can take for granted even on a dual carriageway or freeway with a barrier between the two directions.)

When I am in the US or Europe and driving I try to keep myself feeling uncomfortable because then I know I cannot just take things for granted. When I do start feeling comfortable, then I make mistakes. It is the same about business in India: when I start thinking I am unconsciously doing the correct things I am invariably not. Just try to remain uncomfortable.

There are some adaptations that you can adopt when in India — and when dealing with India and Indian business people — that can make a huge difference to your state of mind. The first adaptation — and actually the second, third and the rest of the series if the truth be known — is time. If you understand time in India, you will survive.

Having worked for an American corporation in India, the contrast between Indian understanding of time and the three month treadmill that is the Wall Street analysts' straitjacket was always in my face. My nadir in understanding occurred some eighteen months into my role when I asked the then country manager what had happened to the order that he promised would be with me by the 14th October now that it was mid way into November. He looked at me, at first puzzled, then he appeared to have a seizure. I had obviously been asking something that just did not make any sense however hard he tried to understand me. I asked him again and said he had promised the order for a month earlier. He looked back at me, genuinely puzzled, and said: "And?"

Now that India is being integrated into global business more and more, it is relatively unusual for a western company to have such a problem with time when dealing with offshoring. Entering the Indian market will remove that smoke screen of understanding and you will be at the cutting edge of a different experience of time.

Time is very much the immediate moment. Next week is something that any Indian can comprehend, of course. It just does not make any sense to do so. The watchword is to sort something *now*. While this seems highly positive — and it can be — it is also a trap for the unwary. You can meet the most senior people today if you need to. Just phone and ask for an appointment.

I have had what seemed to me to be ludicrous conversations with personal assistants and even very senior managers when trying to talk to the managing director or chief executive. I have been told firmly that I just cannot see the CEO now as it is impossible and he is out of the office. When I have said, in reply, as I learned to do, that I did not actually want to see the person now but in three hour's time, the whole situation has changed. In fact — what could be more natural? Of course you can see the CEO then.

For a westerner experienced in making an appointment to see a board member in two month's time this seems difficult to comprehend. The downside in this is immediately obvious: whatever the CEO had booked that afternoon will obviously not take place — as you will have taken the spot over. Indeed, appointments made much more than twenty four hours ahead will have a doubtful existence in India except in your diary.

The real downside, however, is elsewhere, as you will rapidly adapt to changing your work schedule to meet this type of instant gratification. (I have often thought that all those time management companies in the West would have a field day in India just by publishing two pages — the first marked *Today* and the second *Tomorrow*. There would be none of the printing issues about changing the day of the week to match the changing calendar and by printing, say, 100 of the *Today* sheets to every one of the *Tomorrow* pages, they would address the entire market.) The point of this paragraph is that because today is so important it will inevitably occur that you will get a decision for today.

It can be just that: valid only for today.

This is a more serious issue for companies selling into the Indian domestic market than those that are offshoring because they will be making plans on the basis of the decisions made, in general, by people with less under-standing of the force of a decision in the West. You will take a decision as meaning *because of a variety of reasons something will happen*. To an Indian business person, it merely means something between fobbing you off and having some sort of temporary holding position.

The only effective way round this is to ensure that you fortify the decision with a whole series of actions that are agreed and are in writing, and that you formulate this plan at the same meeting as the one where you agree a decision. There is just no room for suggesting that you will come back to your opposite number with a process to put the decision into effect. You just have to do it then and there. What you will find is that the decision will start to become more ethereal the more you try to pin it down. This might seem like a disaster, but it does mean that you will be getting closer and closer to a real decision and a time scale that you can live with.

The perception of time has so many ramifications in India that you will have to think through the implications. You may be used to having your sales people tell you what their plans are for the week. No point. You may wonder why what would have been a one hour meeting in the West takes two hours, starts half an hour after it was supposed to finish, and is concluded in the sales person's report by a general agreement that is quite unspecified. You will wonder a long time.

And just when you think that Indian perception of time is hopeless and something you can hardly deal with, an order that you gave up forecasting six months ago will be signed and this will make you think it can be fath-omed — even if the data you have to date is too flawed for you to make sense of it.

Then just imagine what it feels like when you have come to terms with the Indian sense of time and it is starting to make sense, and head office phones you at around ten thirty at night if you are a European or a UK com-pany and around two in the morning if you are east coast American because it is four or so in the afternoon and they would like an update. At that point not one perception of time, neither Indian, European nor American, makes any sense.

But at least you will now be up and running — and learning. I have often been asked about the qualities that you should look for in appointing an expatiate to run an Indian operation. In previous chapters I have looked at this issue seriously and formally. The abiding answer is, however, someone who is fascinated by the contrast between what is apparently recognisable and what is fundamentally strange. If you can find that person — you will be there.

And once you are up and running, you have to stay ahead of the competition. Here I am not talking about the immediate competition that you will have from entering the Indian market. Much of how to deal with that is in my earlier chapter where I looked at creating the go-to-market plan. I am focused at this point on competition from western companies entering the market.

I have pointed out the difficulties of entering the market and the barriers to entry that mean that once you have got over them you have quite a degree of protection. Nonetheless your western competitors will obviously watch you and your progress and will try to enter the market once they see you are successful.

While you have first mover advantage, they have second mover advantage and will no doubt be able to learn from any mistakes you have made. They will also be tapping into a set of professional services and people who will have had more experience of assisting companies entering the market — if only by helping you. Having mainly worked with companies that were first movers — obviously because there are few companies that have successfully entered the market yet — I have puzzled over whether there are any special issues about India or whether it is the standard practices of entering a market and protecting yourself from competition that should dictate how you behave. My answer is that in general do what you would normally do — but keep one extra factor in mind, and, if it is your normal practice anyway, prioritise it.

The general good practices revolve around supplementing your product and services offer. I know the arguments about focus and they are indeed valid, but protecting your market position is made much easier if you can act aggressively in the market by bolstering the product and service offer. In short — make yourself stickier and stickier for your customers — so it becomes more difficult for another company to reproduce much of what you do in the market. My general advice in India is only to do this when you realise that there is a threat coming but to plan for it as soon as you feel that you have made sufficient progress to contemplate next steps. Have the plan ready, in other words. It may be that you will add extra products to some of the services you offer, or add services to the products.

The planning cannot take place before you are present in the market, at least in my understanding because it needs to be based on market research. Thus, if every sales encounter or marketing opportunity is used to ask what else the potential customer would want to make your offering more acceptable, you will start to build the plan.

Hence my sales meetings and the focus on new facts and understanding about our clients.

The most important part of what you do in India in order to protect any market position you have created is to work on your network. Do not rest until you have good professional relationships across the broad swathe of Indian business in your locale, taking in the bureaucrats in the various government offices — and, in general, your relationship with them will be more important than with the politicians — and do not just consider your own business niche.

You probably would not have any brothers-in-law in India, nor cousins either, and you will need surrogates for them in everything you do. This is quite important in the West to varying degrees in each country, but in India it is the best protection you can get. Infiltrate as many networks as possible and make yourself a useful person if you can. One way that you can do this, if all else fails, is that you can provide back up documentation for any Indian business people who want to travel to a western country on business, including, for example, invitation letters. These apparently small things can go a long way to endearing you and embedding you in the local business environment.

In terms of value think, for example, how useful it might be to have an early warning that another enterprise in your market space is asking for permission to buy land or build an office. That plan you had been developing to counter this threat can be examined and brought into play at the earliest opportunity.

I have always seen competition as useful, as it creates a bigger market and audience for what I am focused on. That has not prevented me from wanting to know what the competition is up to before they start — and placing my resources accordingly.

In India your eyes and ears will be your network. Create it. Deliver value to it. Benefit from it. Think like an Indian — whatever head office has to say about it when your next forecast is proved to be rather out of kilter with a different set of time perceptions.

And add about six months — or 100%, whichever is the larger — to any forecast you are given in India by anyone connected with sales.

TWELVE

INDIA TOMORROW

The journey that we have made in this book does not stop here for a variety of reasons and in a variety of ways. India is developing in unexpected and difficult directions. It will not be a smooth transition from India today to India tomorrow — and those of us who have watched India over the last decade or so know at least one thing: it will be unexpected. My objective is to look at what sort of anticipation is prudent and how to weather the inevitable storms.

The main issue is whether this current development frenzy in India is a bubble — something like the process in Japan, which imploded in stagnation and retrenchment just when global business people were beginning to think that the Japanese model was a different paradigm.

Even using a word like *frenzy* which I chose deliberately is highly indicative of a different perspective. There is no way that India is able to avoid the pitfalls of too rapid development or too slow development because both represent dangers. In short I am an enthusiast for India and the opportunities — the opportunity — it represents in the global market today and in the future but I am also aware that it will not be immediate and it may stutter.

I think the demographics and the Indian trader mentality are too strong for there to be a permanent injury to India's climb to centre of the world's economic stage. On the other hand, there are all the other issues that can trip up the unwary.

Broad-based education provision in India is too patchy and too focused in the wrong direction for it to give any comfort to people in the West, let alone in India. While the best schools and colleges are world class and the elite, which is getting larger rapidly, receives a world class education, female literacy is still both low and falling behind the plans the governments in India have. Female literacy is the silver bullet. You educate a male and you equip him for the world; you educate a girl and you prepare a family for a different way of life. Mothers, especially in India, are the centre of the family and if you educate the girls you create the awareness of the importance of education for the next generation. Yet female education falls behind male education in virtually every state in India.

From education follows smaller families, greater productivity, a better balance between the sexes. It is not for nothing that the one real demographic time bomb in India is focused on the growing imbalance in the poorer states between boys and girls — with infanticide of girl babies one of the major scandals and abortion of female foetuses a commoner practice than admitted generally. Education is not the only answer to these and other such ills, but education is a powerful weapon and one that should be closer to the heart of the Indian government.

There is corruption ranging from the rather insignificant but, nevertheless worrying, low level payments to ensure documents are transferred through a labyrinthine system, to the extreme levels where contracts are bought and sold. Eradicating corruption when it is endemic and tolerated at the highest level — which rather undermines any attempts to remove it at the lowest level — is going to be hard. While it exists to the degree it does, it will seriously hamper India's development.

The very infrastructure that represents such a huge opportunity for western companies in India is creaking already and the way that planning is carried out and development executed is so ramshackle that India is strangling itself with its own development as it is proceeding without the concomitant roads, electricity and water.

The other area that does give some people cause for concern in terms of the sustainability of Indian booming growth is wage inflation. For a new company entering the Indian market it is obviously something of a bonus as disposable incomes are fuelled by this. On the other hand, hot spots within the Indian economy mean that in some areas wage inflation is threatening to price India out of certain service markets worldwide. My words are cautious as it is not happening yet, but I do know that there is more concern within India about inflation of wages and spiralling costs than there was even two years ago. At the moment there is no danger of the wage gap being narrowed too much but by 2015 there are real indications that some sectors of the market will be perilously close. If Indian companies adapt well to this, by, for example, moving up the value chain even faster than they have been doing, this may not be an issue for the economy of the country.

On the other hand it is a danger.

This leads into an analysis of where India will be by 2015, 2025 and even 2050. In the strange sort of way that predictions work it is probably safer to think about 2050 than 2015. By 2050 changes and setbacks will have evened out much of the potential growth in India so that the odd recession or failure to grow at a predicted rate will be less important than the overall growth during the period. As long as there are not sustained wars or catastrophic results from global warming or some other natural disasters and the world economy continues to grow, if not continuously then at least continually, India will do very well. At the very least India will be a significant economic power by 2050 and such an important part of the global economy that it will create trends as well as respond to them. It is likely that the tentacles of Indian business will have penetrated most of the neighbouring countries as the subcontinent stays ahead of the global services market by moving lower value work offshored from the West offshore from India to a vast range of countries.

There are some wags who point to the running of a call centre in Belfast in Ireland by an Indian company, as evidence that already India has identified low cost countries in the West. It is far more complex than that, but a useful perspective. Indian companies are opening centres right across the old eastern Europe and going further east too. By 2050 these companies will be significantly more entrenched and capable of shifting work at will.

The Indian economy is currently buttressed to no small part by remittances from expatriate Indians working all around the globe and not least in the Gulf. By 2050 the Indian economy will be further secured by the profits Indian companies make throughout the world. In this very long term, India will not only be an attractive market but one that any global companies — and those with global pretensions — will have to be in.

By 2025 India will be securely on track to reach this 2050 vision of being one of the top three economies in the world. It will already be a market in which most global companies and medium sized companies from the West will be well established.

The key to an understanding of India in 2025 is not projections of life continuing as it looks at present but to imagine the dislocations that are necessary if India is to achieve the economic heights. To get there India will not be able to afford the unproductive and extraordinarily frustrating lack of a decent infrastructure. Logistics will have to be as little a part of the consciousness of the average Indian business person as it is in the West. We take it for granted that we can ship goods. In India there is no such comfort in the ability to do so. By 2025 that confidence and thoughtlessness will have to be part of the economic backdrop. To get there will cause internal disruption on a major scale — and any such disruption may be an opportunity for western companies or it could make life temporarily unpleasant.

Growth in India between 2015 and 2025 may average less than the 8% or 9% that we are beginning to take for granted, nevertheless it will have to be above western trend levels if India is to reach escape velocity for its very poor and provide a stable political scene that will encourage growth and the development of the market. Again it focuses on education and in all likelihood the availability of health care.

Between now and 2015 there are bound to be shocks to the body politic in India and there may well be lower growth in some years. It would not be out of place to consider political disruption as we see tectonic shifts in attitudes within India.

It may be that there will be great shifts of people to the cities, and we will see a massive urbanisation of India as happened in every developing industrial country, and is happening in China. Nowadays, however, there is a counter to the magnetic growth of cities that has accompanied most countries' transition from an agrarian economy. India may be the first country that truly benefits from the Internet and the mobile phone and may be able to avoid the move to the city. If, as we know to be the case, service jobs which can be accomplished in the next office with the door shut can probably be accomplished anywhere where there is connectivity, there is no reason why India should not see jobs transferred to the villages.

That is if there is the education force in the country to effect the change that is most needed.

The likelihood is, however, that the cities will grow stronger — not just bigger. They will be built and rebuilt to accommodate growth — and the opportunities for western companies with western know how will grow alongside the companies with physical goods to sell.

I see 2015 as a transitional point in India and in the development of its market. It is also as far forward as one can reasonably judge what currently observed trends will produce. The key issue is when there will be pay parity between the West and India. This will not take away India's competitive edge as much as some observers may care to believe because already the Indian labour market at the top end is equally if not better skilled as sections of the western labour forces. Contracts are already being won in India not just on price, and sometimes not on price at all. Wage parity will however have a huge impact on the market in India and the opportunities that there are.

There will still be a large number of absolutely poor people in India by 2015 and the vast majority of the population will be comparatively poor. There is plenty of potential in that fact for civil unrest and political upheavals especially when the vector between rich people's income and poor people's income grows larger. That could be coupled with the real opportunities that exist for religious strife and some of the inter-caste problems that still exist.

The point is that it will not be a continuous upward curve of development. There may be further bubbles.

My only counter to this is that many of us watched the Y2K issue with great interest. I never think similarities or parallels are all that powerful in history, because each event is of its own kind, but how India recovered from what many people rightly saw as a possible issue is instructive.

A great deal of western concern with the year 2000 code breakdown was assuaged by employing what was at that time very low-cost Indian programming resources to check and re-write the code. The industry grew very fast during 1998 and 1999 specifically focused on this one phenomenon. You can see how this could easily be translated into a concern about what would happen when the major stimulus to the market passed — as it inevitably did on 1 January 2000.

There was quite a slowdown in the Indian information technology industry in 2000. Yet what happened is that the market for Indian technology skills started to grow again very quickly and by mid year there was no suggestion of more than a temporary hiccough. In fact, what happened was that the Y2K issue had highlighted the potential for Indian offshoring of systems development and while there was an immediate hiatus as 2000 began, when demand grew it was much faster than expected as more people and companies had been exposed to the advantages of India.

In addition, my own view is that there is such a solid base now to offshoring of information technology and business processes that any shocks to the growth will be absorbed. There will quite naturally be breaks in the continuous upward spiral but the spiral will continue.

There is another major factor which will strengthen the solid growth of India and this is the return of some of the diaspora of Indians round the globe. For centuries Indians have left India for other parts of Asia, Africa and the Gulf in the search for work and prosperity. In the last thirty or so years they have been going to the US primarily and some of them to the UK. Some have arrived in the UK for example, by the circuitous route of East Africa first. The most famous example is when Idi Amin, the Ugandan dictator threw out all, or as many as he could find, of the people of Asian origin in Uganda.

In India these people are known as PIOs — people of Indian origin — as distinct from NRIs — non-resident Indians. For a long time NRIs were highly regarded by Indian governments, especially because of their remittances of money to India, which bolstered the domestic economy over the years. In contrast, PIOs were largely ignored or unconsidered.

In about 2001 the Indian government woke up to the value of PIOs, and all sorts of special cases were created to give PIOs exceptional status. When you think of all the millionaires of Indian origin scattered round the globe, this would seem an obvious move to have made but it did not happen without the usual Indian confusion and controversy.

Nevertheless, as a result of the Indian government's interest in PIOs, there has been much more interest among PIOs in India and its development. There has been a great deal of PIO investment in India and Indian business. There are even examples of PIOs, who may never have previously been to India discovering the attractiveness of India for business and what some people regard as a return to India for them. Since they had never previously been there, *return* is obviously not the right word.

This small current of PIOs returning has been complemented by a huge return of the diaspora — the NRIs who had left to better themselves in the West or, at least west of India. Wherever I am in the world I try to talk to people who are NRIs, partly to gauge their understanding of India but usually to understand whether they will return — genuinely *a return*, of course in their case — to India. I cannot judge the numbers who actually will, but the vast majority do want to return.

I see this as a huge cushion for the Indian economy for the future and enough of my acquaintances, friends and business associates have returned to India over the last few years for me to know that this is a secure and increasing trend. People whose children have been born and educated in the West have gone back or just gone. I have mentioned before that this significant trend is not going to create a mass market, but it does help to create a market with international awareness and a propensity to want western goods and services, with the special cachet they have.

My own company in Chennai is jointly owned with me by a business associate who had been in the UK for many years and who deliberately went back to India. Selwyn is one of the biggest advocates of the future of India that I know and he slips easily between an Indian consciousness and a western perspective and it is that quality that I find very valuable in India today for all companies that want to set up and sell into that market. Selwyn and I still have different perceptions but there is enough common ground because of his engagement with the West and my engagement with India for us to work extremely well together although it is quite paradoxical. He, being Indian, routinely underestimates costs in India and is continuously surprised by how long things take to happen. I am just astonished whenever we manage to accomplish anything at all. This means that my disappointments, just when I have lulled myself into a Selwyn-induced sense of well-being and confidence, are doubly hard.

I am especially conscious of the moment we were about to go live with our international telecommunications, which had taken months and months to achieve despite it being absolutely straightforward *and no issues*. A digger managed to cut through the fibre that had been specially laid to our door. It did not, being India, just cut through it — although that was how it was represented to me immediately — but managed to pull it up and destroy it over something like half a kilometre. To this day I have this picture of a digger driver wondering what on earth the cat's cradle of fibre optics was doing there — and probably wondering what on earth it was.

If I have one further message about India — it is always be surprised if things go off well.

My message from this is broader than the individual. When you get to India and start embedding yourself in the culture, you will soon become aware of the leaven that Indians with western experience bring. Just do not imagine that they are westerners. In the same way that I always tell my Indian colleagues that they must not for one moment imagine that I am Indian even though I can behave in an Indian way and do understand something of the culture, Indians may be westernised but they are still Indian.

There is nothing like what amounts to inbuilt suspicion, not about motives but about their certainties, to help preserve the best relationship between westerners and Indian business people.

The corollary of this is that something I mentioned above is also important. There are all sorts of organisations of Indian business people in the West. The +91 Group — named after the international telephone number for India, and TiE — The Indus Entrepreneur — are but two of the many. You can find out a great deal by tapping into the resources you have in your own country. My greatest enjoyment about these groups, however, is the difference in perception and understanding both ways.

Be wary of the insights — but any insights are still worth quite a lot of hard experience. By way of illustration I am always struck by the enthusiasm for India and Indian business that these groups evince which is in stark contrast with the views expressed by any individuals. If this sounds confusing to you, just imagine what it is like when you are actually engaged in these matters. To be told collectively that India represents the last frontier of business excitement and also that it is the graveyard of ambition because of the intense bureaucracy and corruption is quite disorienting.

Do not trust the speakers in either sense.

I suppose the area where I get most confused in India is on some of the green issues. Indian governments have faced squarely up to some of the issues by saying they will do nothing about them until the US shows that it is taking a lead. On the other, conditions can get so bad that the politicians have to take a stance, even if the focus is not on greenness but on the sheer impossibility of breathing. A few years ago there was a great moment when all the motorised rickshaws had to be converted to liquid petroleum gas or LPG. The great changeover date arrived with all the engines converted, and Delhi was about to heave a collective sigh and inhale some relatively unpolluted air.

The one trouble was that while all the preparations were in place, there was one, tiny oversight. No one had thought of ensuring that there were sufficient pumps for the LPG in the service stations. Consequently there were endless queues of three wheelers at every service station for days and days and days. I was solemnly informed, however, that those that had enough fuel to let their engines tick over while waiting were, in fact, very green and not polluting the atmosphere. That felt very Indian.

The truth is that India is nowhere near China in terms of carbon emissions, but it is growing fast and there is an acute awareness in India, even if it does not quite get to legislation, that something has to be done. The very nature of Indian culture suggests that it will take a positive route forward on green issues and there will be a market for companies that have goods, services and knowledge in this area. My caveat is that this will take a good deal of time to permeate the infrastructure — and I do not just mean the political levels. Alongside the Indian ability to perceive the necessity for a green agenda — and for it to be very close to Indian hearts throughout the organised sector of business — there is also that Indian ability to sidestep every regulation known to man.

It is too early at the moment to enter the market on a green manifesto, but it is enough of a strong undercurrent to keep it firmly in mind.

Knowing when to enter the Indian market is the most important fact. Up until mid 2006 we were advising our clients to keep an eye on the Indian domestic market but not to enter it unless the company naturally had a great deal of patience. It would not require deep pockets necessarily but it would mean a great deal of treading water. Through 2006 we began to advise clients that the time was becoming ripe to take a decision. What we were looking at was a number of key indicators that were not necessarily related but which did give insights into what was happening. We were looking in general terms across the whole economy, and taking snap shots of the individual sectors to see when was the right time to move.

A major indicator for me was the development of multiplex cinemas. Taken in isolation it is of course completely absurd to base an economic model on such a development but taken in the perspective of the development of retail malls, the growth of the international logistics companies in India, and the continuous growth in the offshoring of business processes, it said something very powerful. For me it meant that India was going beyond the Bollywood cinema experience into a world of entertainment centres with all that that means in terms of other outlets grouped round them, from fast food to fashion shops. It made me look at the Indian domestic market in new ways and to see the way that the possibilities for B2B and B2C western companies were changing.

The key signs are also the more normal ones for those businesses aware that they must enter the Indian market but are not sure about timing. The first is the regulatory environment. As India moves inexorably away from child labour, from sweat shops, from an unorganised economy to an organised economy with proper respect for corporation taxes and Value Added Tax — I take it that respect for income taxes will remain as low as it does in most western countries — and away from state-centric purchase taxes, the opportunities for western companies increase. In many cases we decry regulation in the West, but it has prepared western companies for the future in India which the local Indian companies will have difficulty in dealing with.

In this way regulation will stimulate the demand for western goods and services and it will also give western companies an unfair advantage as the western mindset is to work within regulations whereas the Indian mindset is to circumvent. As governments also move to reduce corruption within the IAS, partly by outsourcing some of the functions in government partly by directly addressing the fatal flaw in the Indian economy of the government sector being the most highly sought after, there will be a need for western corporate governance.

In short, look at India through the lens of the normal signs of a healthy economy in your sector, but also take account of the huge changes in consumption patterns, income patterns and attitudes amongst Indians to quality of life.

Look at the figures for literacy and numeracy. That will be a major indicator about the maturity of the consumer market. Look at birth rates by individual states and see how these are influencing the growth in the market. Look at industrial production figures, of course. Look at the Sensex Index on the Bombay Stock Exchange. Look at real estate prices. Look at the development of services industries. Look at employment rates, not only the percentage of those in employment but at the gross figures for employment, especially in the non-agricultural sector, taking into account how non-labour intensive the Indian services industries are. Look at the per capita income figures. Examine closely the statistics that you can see about India — always trusting the trend rather than the gross figures. Look at published figures for industrial injuries, bearing in mind that the increase may well reveal a greater regulatory regime rather than a growth in accidents. Look at the tourist figures for tourists coming *from* the sub-continent. Look at any available figures for the return of the diaspora. Take note, too, of the number of western companies that are beginning to talk about entering the Indian market. Watch how many western companies are actually investing in India. Look at the foreign direct investment figures for India — and how they are growing not only in gross figures but against the huge foreign direct investment figures for China. Look at any joint initiatives India takes with China: the focus they have will tell you much about the state of the Indian economy.

What you will find is that there is real interest and real growth and real ignorance about India. Ignorance and fear are the hurdles to entering the market — and the hurdles that you can use once you are in India to stop your competitors.

As I have said for years now, the only thing to do is go to India and see it for yourself. Do not ignore the huge inequalities, do not ignore the bureaucracy and do not ignore the frustrations, but do also see the opportunity that is developing before our eyes. Remember how important the Indian economy was up to 1800 — and see how it is re-asserting that capability and position. Think about growing your company at 10% per year by having a presence in India.

Be aware that whatever you do, Indian companies are beginning to enter your market in more convincing ways. Large swathes of the European steel industry is already controlled by an Indian company. High profile car companies have been taken over by Indians. More and more companies in the pharmaceutical field are being bought up by Indians. You will see your home market attacked by Indians. It seems only fair that you should be able to have a go at them in their own backyard.

I share some of the worries of the political classes throughout the West that India will be an opportunity that much of western business will ignore. I cannot tell whether India will be right for you now or in two or three years' time. I do know however that you have to have an informed opinion about whether you should be there, otherwise the West will lose a huge opportunity and we will all be the poorer for that loss, and that includes Indians and westerners.

I do not mean that we will necessarily stop growing and will stop increasing in wealth, as foreign direct investment from India will keep our markets going. I do mean that we will have lost the greatest opportunity that the world has seen to be in at the start of the biggest change in the global economy ever.

Should you go to China first? Should you tackle Russia or Brazil? Are there any other developing markets that you should address first? If you do not know the answer, please weigh up India against the opportunities each of these present and make a decision.

Should you stay at home and let the growth in Indian companies in your market take away your competitive edge? That seems to me to be the stark opposite choice to finding out about India and its domestic market.

I always fight shy of charlatans who insist that you do not have an alternative. What I am hoping this book has shown you is that you do have intrinsically an alternative to investing in India but that you have no alternative to making a decision about where India does or does not figure in your business planning.

And by the way — just go there to see. You may fall in love with it — as I did — or you may hate it.

You will not remain indifferent.

LIST OF WEBSITES
AND RESOURCES

Union Government

Official Website: www.india.gov.in
Department of Commerce: www.commerce.nic.in

States

No.	State	State Website	Union Government State Website
1.	Andhra Pradesh	www.aponline.gov.in	http://www.india.gov.in/ knowindia/st_andhra.php
2.	Arunachal Pradesh	www.arunachalpradesh.nic.in	http://www.india.gov.in/ knowindia/st_arunachal.php
3.	Assam	www.assamgovt.nic.in	http://www.india.gov.in/ knowindia/st_assam.php
4.	Bihar	www.bihar.ws or www.gov.bih.nic.in	http://www.india.gov.in/ knowindia/st_bihar.php
5.	Chhattisgarh	www.chhattisgarh.nic.in	http://www.india.gov.in/ knowindia/st_chhattisgarh.php

(*Continued*)

(*Continued*)

No.	State	State Website	Union Government State Website
6.	Goa	www.goagovt.nic.in	http://www.india.gov.in/knowindia/st_goa.php
7.	Gujarat	www.gujaratindia.com	http://www.india.gov.in/knowindia/st_gujurat.php
8.	Haryana	www.haryana.gov.in	http://www.india.gov.in/knowindia/st_haryana.php
9.	Himachal Pradesh	www.himachal.nic.in	http://www.india.gov.in/knowindia/st_himachal.php
10.	Jammu and Kashmir	www.jammukashmir.nic.in	http://www.india.gov.in/knowindia/st_jammukashmir.php
11.	Jharkhand	www.jharkhand.nic.in	http://www.india.gov.in/knowindia/st_jharkhand.php
12.	Karnataka	www.karnataka.com	http://www.india.gov.in/knowindia/st_karnataka.php
13.	Kerala	www.kerala.com	http://www.india.gov.in/knowindia/st_kerala.php
14.	Madhya Pradesh	www.mp.nic.in	http://www.india.gov.in/knowindia/st_madhyapradesh.php
15.	Maharashtra	www.maharashtra.gov.in	http://www.india.gov.in/knowindia/st_maharashtra.php
16.	Manipur	www.manipur.nic.in	http://www.india.gov.in/knowindia/st_manipur.php
17.	Meghalaya	www.meghalaya.nic.in	http://www.india.gov.in/knowindia/st_meghalaya.php
18.	Mizoram	www.mizoram.nic.in	http://www.india.gov.in/knowindia/st_mizoram.php
19.	Nagaland	www.nagaland.nic.in	http://www.india.gov.in/knowindia/st_nagaland.php
20.	Orissa	www.orissagov.nic.in	http://www.india.gov.in/knowindia/st_orissa.php
21.	Punjab	www.punjabgovt.nic.in	http://www.india.gov.in/knowindia/st_punjab.php
22.	Rajasthan	www.rajasthan.gov.in	http://www.india.gov.in/knowindia/st_rajasthan.php

(*Continued*)

(Continued)

No.	State	State Website	Union Government State Website
23.	Sikkim	www.sikkim.gov.in	http://www.india.gov.in/ knowindia/st_sikkim.php
24.	Tamil Nadu	www.tn.gov.in	http://www.india.gov.in/ knowindia/st_tamilnadu.php
25.	Tripura	www.tripura.nic.in	http://www.india.gov.in/ knowindia/st_tripura.php
26.	Uttarakhand	www.gov.ua.nic.in	http://www.india.gov.in/ knowindia/st_uttaranchal.php
27.	Uttar Pradesh	www.upgov.nic.in	http://www.india.gov.in/ knowindia/st_uttarpradesh.php
28.	West Bengal	www.wbgov.com	http://www.india.gov.in/ knowindia/st_westbengal.php

Union Territories

No.	Territory	Territory Website	Union Government Territory Website
1.	Andaman and Nicobar Islands	www.and.nic.in	http://www.india.gov.in/ knowindia/ut_andaman.php
2.	Chandigarh	www.chandigarh.nic.in	http://www.india.gov.in/ knowindia/ut_chandigarh.php
3.	Dadra and Nagar Haveli	www.dnh.nic.in	http://www.india.gov.in/ knowindia/ ut_dadranagarhaveli.php
4.	Daman and Diu	www.daman.nic.in	http://www.india.gov.in/ knowindia/ut_damandiu.php
5.	Delhi	www.delhigovt.nic.in	http://www.india.gov.in/ knowindia/ut_delhi.php
6.	Lakshadweep	www.lakshadweep.nic.in	http://www.india.gov.in/ knowindia/ut_lakshadweep.php
7.	Puducherry	www.pon.nic.in	http://www.india.gov.in/ knowindia/ut_pondicherry.php

Newspapers

Asian Age
Daily coverage of India and South Asia

Asian News International (ANI)
New Delhi based South Asian multimedia news agency providing news coverage from India and South Asia

Business Standard
Major financial newspaper

Economic Times
Daily business newspaper from the Times of India group

Express India
News portal publishing several major Indian newspapers

Financial Express
Provides financial and industrial news, stock market reports

Hard News
Political Indian magazine, partner of the eminent French monthly *Le Monde Diplomatique*

Hindu
National daily newspaper, based in Madras

Hindu Group of Publications
Online presentation of many Indian newspapers and magazines

Hindustan Times
Major daily newspaper from Delhi

India Daily
News, primarily aimed at foreign and expatriate audience

India Monitor
Online news service covering Indian subcontinent

Indian Express
Delhi based daily

Milli Gazette
Newspaper for Indian Muslims

NDTV.com
News site of Delhi-based TV offering live video reports

New Indian Express
Newspaper with focus on the southern states

Outlook India
Weekly newsmagazine known for in-depth, investigative reporting

Radiance Viewsweekly
India's oldest Muslim English weekly

Rediff
Indian news and entertainment portal

Samachar.com
Provides aggregates news from all major Indian newspapers

Statesman
One of India's oldest newspaper, based in Calcutta

Tehelka
Alternative news magazine

Telegraph
Calcutta-based national daily

Times of India
Quality national daily from Delhi

Week
Weekly magazine with critical reporting of national news

Local Indian Newspapers

Agra News
Ahmedabad (Gujarat)
Assam Tribune (Guwahati)
Central Chronicle (Bhopal)
Chitralekha (online weekly aimed at Gujaratis)
Daily Excelsior (Jammu)
Deccan Chronicle (Hyderabad)
Deccan Herald (Bangalore)
Deepika (Kerala)
Dharitri (Bhubaneswar)
Ganashtaki (Calcutta)
Greater Kashmir (Srinigar)
Gujarat Plus
Gujjuweb (Ahmedabad)
Kashmir Monitor (Srinagar)
Kashmir Observer (Srinigar)
Kashmir Times (Jammu)
Kaumudi (Kerala)
Malayala Manorama (Kottayam)
Mid-Day Mumbai
Navhind Times (Panjim)
New Kerala (Kochi)
News Today (Chennai)
Orissa India (Bhubaneswar)
Pioneer (New Delhi)
Pragativadi (Bhubaneswar)
Punjab Newsline (Mohali)
Ranchi Express
Rupaliparda.com — magazine on Assamese entertainment industry

Samachar (Mysore)
Sentinel (Guwahati)
Star of Mysore
Tribune (Chandigarh)

References — Books

Luce E (2007). *In Spite of the Gods: The Strange Rise of Modern India.*
Davies P (2004). *What's This India Business? Offshoring, Outsourcing and the Global Services Revolution.*
Smith D (2007). *The Dragon and the Elephant: China, India and the New World Order.*
Tully M (2007). *India's Unending Journey: Finding Balance in a Time of Change.*
Tully M (1992). *No Full Stops in India.*

Industry

No.	Organisation	Website	Comments
1.	India Brand Equity Foundation	www.ibef.in	The best site for statistics and national insights
2.	Confederation of Indian Industry	www.ciionline.org	Trends
3.	Confederation of Indian Industry Institute of Logistics	www.ciilogistics.com	
4.	Federation of Indian Chambers of Commerce and Industry	www.ficci.com	
5.	The McKinsey Quarterly	www.e-mckinseyquarterly.com	Good, up to date general surveys of India included from time to time

Trade Directories and Useful Sites

No.	Organisation	Website	Comments
1.	Jimtrade.com	www.jimtrade.com	
2.	Trade India	www.tradeindia.com	
3.	IndiaTradeZone.com	www.indiatradezone.com	
4.	eIndia Business	www.eindiabusiness.com	
5.	Trade Mart India	www.trade.indiamart.com	

Trade Associations

No.	Organisation	Website	Comments
1.	National Association of Software and Services Companies	www.nasscom.org	The main trade association for IT and BPO
2.	Directory of Trade Associations	www.indianchild.com/ trade_associations_ business_organisations_ india.htm	A directory of trade associations

INDEX